*Masters of Equitation
on Trot*

Masters of Equitation on Trot

Compiled by
Martin Diggle

Trafalgar Square Publishing

First Published in the United States of America in 2001 by
Trafalgar Square Publishing, North Pomfret, Vermont 05053

ISBN 1-57076-197-3

LOC#: Library of Congress Card Number: 2001086835

All extracts from *Dressage A Study of the Finer Points of Riding* by Henry Wynmalen
are reproduced by permission of the Wilshire Book Company (California, USA);
from *Riding Logic* by Wilhelm Müseler by permission of The Random House
Group Ltd.; from *The Complete Training of Horse and Rider* by Alois Podhajsky by
permission of The Sportsman's Press; from *The Gymnasium of the Horse* by Gustav
Steinbrecht by permission of Xenophon Press (Cleveland Heights, Ohio, USA).

The following photographs and illustrations are also reproduced by permission:
Sequence of steps at the trot (page 23), from Podhajsky's *The Complete Training of
Horse and Rider* by permission of The Sportsman's Press; Ordinary working trot of
young horse (page 32) and Felix Bürkner on Bober (page 69), from Müseler's
Riding Logic by permission of The Random House Group Ltd.; Outward signs of
tractability and insufficient tractability (page 79), from Knopfhart's *Dressage A
Guidebook for the Road to Success* by permission of Half Halt Press, Inc. (PO Box 67,
Boonsboro, Maryland 21756, USA).

Jacket photograph of the compiler by permission of Mike Freeman

The compiler and publisher acknowledge all of these generous permissions with
thanks. Despite our best efforts we have been unable to trace ownership of the
copyright of some material included in this book. If anyone feels that they have a
claim, please contact the publisher.

Design by Nancy Lawrence
Series compiler Martin Diggle

Printed in Hong Kong

Contents

Introduction to the Masters of Equitation on Dressage Series

When we first discover a new pursuit, most of us explore it with more enthusiasm than science. This is necessarily so, since our desire to participate greatly exceeds our understanding of the principles involved. It is when we begin actively to seek a greater understanding of these principles that we can be sure that we have acquired a genuine new interest, and are not simply indulging a passing fad.

In our quest for knowledge, we look first to the nearest and most obvious sources. If our new interest is riding, we acquire an instructor, listen (hopefully) to what we are told, and begin to question the apparent paradoxes of equitation as they unfold. With time, our field of information broadens; we learn what our instructor has been told by his or her instructor, we begin to follow the exploits of top riders in the different disciplines, and we even start to read books.

It is at some point along this path that we start to realise just what a wealth of knowledge we have at our disposal. We also begin to realise that much of this knowledge is far from new. There is initial surprise when we learn that the elderly gentleman who trains our current idol was, himself, an Olympic medallist – a further surprise that he, in turn, was trained by a cavalry officer famed, in his time, as a leading light of the Cadre Noir. We discover in a book written forty or fifty years ago ideas of which we were unaware, and then marvel at the extensive references to writers long dead before the author's own birth. We regard, with awe, faded, grainy photographs of riders whose positions – even to our untutored eyes – look positively centaur-like, and we are bemused by ancient diagrams of school movements that make today's dressage tests seem like a hack in the park.

If, at this point, we pause to reflect a little, we start to see this heritage in its true context. It is a common human conceit to believe that we, or our near contemporaries, are the first to discover anything, but this is very rarely true. So far as riding is concerned, it is no exaggeration to say that it is, in absolute terms, less important to us than it was to our ancestors. If we need to prove this point we can consider that, three hundred years ago, a poorly ridden lateral movement might result in decapitation by an enemy sabre. The same movement, ridden today, would result in an 'insufficient' on the test sheet, and a wounded ego.

Of course, it is not the case that all equitation of times past was concerned with the vital necessities of war. Certainly since the renaissance, there have always been people fascinated by the *art* of riding – interestingly, this group includes a number of Masters who were, first and foremost, military men.

It is in the nature of art to give birth to experimentation, innovation and re-interpretation, and it is in the nature of artists to be influenced by – even to borrow from – others, and yet still develop their own styles. Sometimes, in pursuit of new ideas, an acknowledged Master may stray too far down a particular path, causing even his most admiring pupils to question the wisdom of the route, but such instances have a way of triggering the reassessment and consolidation of major principles.

All of these things have happened in equitation, against a background of different types and breeds of horses, and varying equestrian requirements. Not surprisingly, this has given rise to a number of schools, or philosophies, which place different degrees of emphasis on certain principles. By delving into the wealth of literature available, it is possible for the avid reader to discover these philosophies, and draw from them ideas and information which may be of personal value. However, because of the amount of material available, and the need to embark upon a major voyage of discovery, this can be considered an extensive – albeit rewarding – process.

The purpose behind the *Masters of Equitation* series is to gather together, under individual subject headings, many of the key thoughts of eminent equestrians, thus providing a convenient source of reference to their ideas. The reader is invited to research, compare and contrast – and may find a special significance in areas of obvious consensus.

Compiler's Note

In producing this series of books, the aims of the publisher are twofold. First, it is certainly the intention that they should act as reference works, giving readers with specific schooling queries access to the thoughts of many Masters in a single volume.

Second, it is very much hoped that they will act as an appetiser, a stimulus for further reading of the original works cited and, indeed, for Classical equestrian works in general.

With regard to this latter aim, I can foresee that some readers, who have already made a study of the Classics, may search this book in vain for their favourite extract or author. If this happens, I beg such readers' pardon. The truth is, in order to be completely comprehensive, a book such as this would have to quote great swathes of material from very many sources – an undertaking that would exhaust the energies of compiler, publisher and perhaps even the most ardent reader!

Rather than attempt the impossible, I have endeavoured to provide in this series a good cross-section of references from different eras, countries and schools of equestrian thought. It was, indeed, the publisher's express wish that the series should contain a broad overview of various ideas and persuasions and that it should not seek to promote the ideas of one School over another. Some of the quoted material comes from writers who may not be instantly recognised as pre-eminent 'Masters'; these extracts are included for reasons of interest or contrast, or simply because they are apposite.

For those who would welcome a rationale for the material included and omitted, I will attempt to provide one in a brief historical context.

In the first instance, there are no extracts from Xenophon's *The Art of Horsemanship*. By way of explanation, I can do no better than quote from W. Sidney Felton's excellent work, *Masters of Equitation:*

Xenophon's approach to schooling [his humane understanding of the horse] makes it easy to see why he is widely quoted by modern writers on equitation. Indeed, it would seem that many authors feel that they have not adequately established a claim to a knowledge of classical equitation if they do not find an opportunity to refer to Xenophon as the first master of the art of riding...However, in honoring Xenophon as the earliest and hence one of the most significant of a long series of writers on the subject of equitation, we must not lose sight of the fact that educated riding as it exists today has been built up from the contributions of a long line of skilled horsemen over a long period of years. It is remarkable that Xenophon should have expressed so clearly the principles that should govern our approach to...schooling... the horse, but we should not make the mistake of asserting that he was also the master of techniques of riding that did not even come into existence until many centuries after his era.

I should add that I have great personal admiration for Xenophon's humanity and understanding of the horse's psyche, which I believe were not equalled until well beyond the renaissance era. Which brings us to that era, and my reasons for the paucity of quotations from it.

With no evidence to the contrary, it is generally accepted that, throughout the Dark Ages and the medieval period, equitation, in the modern sense, did not exist. Horses were basically compelled to do their riders' bidding, by whatever brutal means were most expedient. The rise, in sixteenth century Italy, of the Neapolitan School, saw the *beginning* of a remarkable change. My reason for emphasising *beginning* is that the renaissance in riding should be seen in the literal sense of the word, a 'rebirth'. To illustrate this point, when Federigo Grisone, the founder of the Neapolitan School, emphasised the importance of the rider's legs in schooling, his suggestion was seized upon as a great innovation and refinement of what had gone before.

It is certainly true that teachers of the School, such as Grisone, Fiaschi and Pignatelli introduced the concept of riding as a science and an art and their influence 'lit the fuse', as it were, for the explosion of equestrian thought that was to follow. However, while their influence (especially that of Pignatelli, through his illustrious pupils from many countries) was immense, the Neapolitan School can be seen as instigating an awakening from the Dark Ages which was both gradual and prolonged. Snapshots of this School are provided, again, by W. Sidney Felton:

What was this new type of riding and schooling which gained such rapid acceptance? First of all, it was a method based on complete subjugation of the horse. Training was often carried on not by one person alone, but by a riding master with one, two or even more assistants. All of these assistants carried whips or rods. And from the short length of time that a whip was reported as lasting, it is evident that they were not merely pointed at the horse...[as] in longeing.

A great deal of work was done with pillars, that is the horse was fastened to a single pillar and worked in a circle around it.

Curb bits were used exclusively and were of a most elaborate design. The riders of that day...had an infinite variety of designs. But all of these bits without exception had one thing in common – that they had very long cheeks and were very severe by any modern standard. And the effect is clearly seen in the pictures illustrating what was then considered proper carriage and proper action, for in our eyes the horses were very much overcollected. Again and again we see horses pictured with their heads as much as thirty degrees behind the vertical and quite apparently behind the bit.

Perhaps it is an unfair inference, but one cannot but wonder whether the horsemen of this period were not afraid of their horses. Certainly they used every possible method of restraint, and extended gaits or even a free...walk on a loose rein had no place in their schooling.

If these reflections seem, to modern readers, to be damning, the writer goes on to make a telling point:

But, while we may find much in the early school riding which we would not wish to follow today, we must not lose sight of the fact that it represented a great step forward from anything which had preceded it...and that it was the foundation for the more modern school riding, particularly in France, which in turn has become the advanced dressage riding of today.

It is likely that several factors contributed to the decline of the Neapolitan School and the ascendancy of the French School. W. Sidney Felton adds his own theory that the early form of School riding...

...had relatively little utilitarian value. It was a very specialized sport or game developed partly for the gratification of the participant but very largely for its spectator appeal. The French Court...provided a much grander stage...than was available in the small [and often warring] Italian principalities...

Two of the founder figures of the French School were Salomon de la Broue and Antoine de Pluvinel, both of whom had studied at the Neapolitan School. De la Broue was the first trainer of his era to use a bridoon rather than a curb bit in the early stages of training. De Pluvinel, a student of Pignatelli, is credited with being the first humane trainer of his era. Although this should be considered in the context of his times, he certainly took account of the horse's powers of reasoning, and understood that the horse does not always resist out of malice, but frequently through lack of understanding.

De Pluvinel was also riding instructor to King Louis XIII, and it was his success, together with that of de la Broue, which caused the French Monarchy to give its support to equitation, founding the School of Versailles, which flourished until the French Revolution. It was this background that produced the figure widely regarded as the most influential in the history of equitation, François Robichon de la Guérinière. W. Sidney Felton describes him thus:

We come now, in the first half of the eighteenth century, to the man who has often been described as the greatest horseman of all time. De la Guérinière, building on the foundation established by de Pluvinel, accomplished what was little short of a revolution. He initiated that artistic freedom of action which is so characteristic of the modern French School and he developed the methods by which that freedom could be obtained...We might fairly call him the first of the modern classical riders. His book,

Ecole de Cavalerie, though published in 1733, is still considered a standard work and is often quoted by students of equitation.

Of course, it is now a very long time since de la Guérinière was writing and teaching. The art and science of equitation have continued to develop on an increasingly international basis, and many great Masters have appeared since his time. For the most part, it is extracts from their works which feature in these pages. It seems to me that de la Guérinière represents a fundamental watershed in equestrian history, and his abiding influence on Classical equitation is the main reason why most of the quotations in this series are 'post-Guérinière'.

One final point, concerning form of words. The Masters quoted in this book wrote in various eras, languages and styles and, in many cases, their work has been subject to translation. Therefore, the reader may notice that word forms and usage appear to vary from one extract to another. Other than this, variations in actual spellings are a consequence of quoting verbatim from both English and American publications.

Introduction to the Masters of Equitation on Trot

Trot is the utilitarian gait; the gait at which much general schooling is carried out. It is most suited to this purpose since it is more impulsive than walk and less complex than canter. As a consequence of the diagonal nature of the gait, all four legs perform an equal amount of work, and the muscles of the back flex and extend alternately on each side of the spine, producing a suppling effect upon the whole body.

If it is to fulfil its role as a suppling and training gait, the trot itself must be of good quality, and should improve and develop as training progresses. Of course, this improvement and development may go far beyond the bounds of even an excellent working trot, to the most spectacular extensions and the ultimate levels of collection, as evidenced in piaffe and passage.

These movements, and the commentaries upon them, will, however, be subjects for further books in this series. In *The Masters of Equitation on Trot*, the emphasis is fundamentally upon the role and development of the working trot.

The Value of the Trot

An important point recognised by the Masters of equitation is that the gaits themselves have a role beyond mere locomotion – correctly employed, they have a key role in the training process. Writing in the early years of the eighteenth century, the great French Master, de la Guérinière, explained the training value of trot with typical clarity. (The M. de la Broue referred to initially is Salomon de la Broue, one of the founder figures of the French School.)

M. de la Broue cannot define a well-trained horse other than by saying that such a horse is supple, obedient, and precise: for if a horse is not entirely free and supple, it cannot obey the will of the rider with ease and grace, and suppleness necessarily produces docility, because the horse then has no difficulty in executing what is commanded. These are, then, the three essential qualities of what is called a *dressed horse*.

The first of these qualities is acquired solely by means of the trot. This is a common belief among all experienced horsemen, of the past as well as the present, and if among them any have rejected the trot without good reason and sought this fundamental suppleness and freedom of movement in a smaller, shorter gait [presumably a reference to archaic forms of over-collection, not simply to walk] they were mistaken; for these qualities be imparted to the horse only by bringing into broad movement all its muscles...

It is by the trot, the most natural gait, that a horse is rendered light to the hand without ruining its mouth, and quickens the limbs without straining them; for in this movement, which is the highest of the natural gaits, the horse's body is supported by two legs, one fore and one hind; which gives the two others ease in being raised, supported and extended forward, and hence imparts a high degree of suppleness to all parts of the body.

François Robichon de la Guérinière *School of Horsemanship*

To these observations, de la Guérinière adds a warning which should echo down to the present day:

The trot is hence, without any question, the basis of all lessons designed to render a horse adept and obedient. But although a thing may be excellent in principle, it must not be abused by trotting a horse for years on end as was formerly a common practice in Italy and is still done in certain countries in which horsemanship enjoys a high esteem. The reason is quite simple: since the perfection of the trot proceeds from the strength of the limbs, that strength and natural vigour, which one must at all costs preserve in a horse, is lost and drained away in heaviness of body and fatigue, the results of a lesson too strenuous and continuous for too long a time. This state also occurs in young horses made to trot on rough or soft ground, which gives rise to thoroughpins, curbs, spavins, and other diseases of the hock, maladies which strike very good horses as a result of the over-exertion of the muscles and tendons by persons who boast of breaking a horse in a short time: it should be called ruination rather than training.

François Robichon de la Guérinière *School of Horsemanship*

Le trot from de la Guérinière's School of Horsemanship.

De la Guérinière's description of the value of trot is endorsed by many great riders down the ages. John Winnett, Olympic rider, long-serving captain of the American dressage team and a great admirer of de la Guérinière, writes:

The trot is the horse's most natural gait, and the touchstone of all training. Before the ultimate development of collection the trot remains the least tiring of the three natural gaits, for both hind and forelegs develop the same amount of kinetic energy, and perform the same amount of work.

He expands on this by further describing the suppling effect of the gait:

The horse is best made supple in the trot, for in this gait the muscles of the back flex and extend alternately on each side of the spine, in rhythm with the diagonal rising and transfer of balance in the gait – and this motion creates a suppling effect upon the whole body.

John Winnett *Dressage as Art in Competition*

The primacy of trot as a schooling gait is further emphasised by others:

Since the trot is the most efficient movement for the gymnasticising of the horse...we have to begin to teach him this gait and work on it until we have a horse that, to quote Bourgelat*, 'trots with impulse, being decontracted and in balance'.

H.L.M. van Schaik *Misconceptions and Simple Truths in Dressage*

(*Claude Bourgelat (1712–79), author of *Le Nouveau Newcastle, ou Nouveau Traité de cavalerie géometrique, théorique et pratique,* manager of the French Riding Academy and founder of the first veterinary school in Lyon.)

It is the trot that is best suited for obtaining and preserving impulsion. At the same time it improves suppleness and develops obedience, for the rider can influence his horse better in the trot than the walk where the natural impulsion is lacking, or in the canter where the horse can easily become tense.

Alois Podhajsky *The Complete Training of Horse and Rider*

Sequence of steps at the trot. From Podhajsky's
The Complete Training of Horse and Rider.

The all-round horseman, Lt. Col. A.L. d'Endrödy, appreciated the trot for its value both in crossing country efficiently and in schooling:

The trot is the most rhythmical and most even pace of locomotion, and for these reasons it is the most suitable for covering long distances reasonably quickly and with relatively little exertion.

In the trot, the animal proceeds by making identical and simultaneous movements with its diagonal legs. In this way the pace, by its simple grouping of movements, and by its natural balance and swing, facilitates the teaching work of the rider and the learning of the horse. Therefore, this is the pace which plays the main role in the horse's schooling.

Lt. Col. A.L. d'Endrödy *Give Your Horse a Chance*

Natural equilibrium of an unmounted horse at a free and easy trot.
From Knopfhart's Fundamentals of Dressage.

Erik Herbermann emphasises the value of trot in schooling both horse and rider:

The bulk of riding should be carried out at the trot. It is the schooling gait for both horse and rider. The work at both the walk and canter will usually progress favourably only once the trot work becomes mature. The trot is more impulsive than the walk. It is the best gait for teaching the horse to balance itself, first on the longe, later under the rider; learning to respond to the activating aids, becoming supple and using its back and hindquarters; and above all, learning to stretch for the rider's hands, which is the foundation for all correct work.

...The rider's seat and position will only develop correctly after much work at the sitting trot without stirrups, including being longed. Generally, once the rider has developed a good seat at the trot, then sitting well to the walk and canter poses few problems. Erik Herbermann *Dressage Formula*

His thoughts regarding the rider are much in accord with those of de la Guérinière, who wrote:

The knowledge of how to position oneself on horseback...is not sufficient of itself: the rider must be able to maintain this posture, a thing more difficult when the horse is in motion. For this reason the wise master adopts the custom of having beginners ride a good deal at the trot, in order to give them a deep seat in the saddle. Nothing surpasses the trot as a gait for the formation of riders. They are in ease at other gaits after such exercise because other gaits are less rough. The practice of working at the trot for five or six months without stirrups is also excellent; the legs thus rest necessarily close to the horse, and the rider learns proper posture and balance thereby.

François Robichon de la Guérinière *School of Horsemanship*

Henry Wynmalen, widely regarded as one of the 'fathers' of British dressage, was a great student of Classical equitation, and shared the general view of trot as the most valuable gait for schooling. He wrote:

All authorities agree that the cultivation of a good trot is basic to the development of balance, and that as such it is the key to all advanced training.

---

and:

The rhythm of the trot is of itself of inestimable value for the horse's athletic development...The trot is the only gait which is absolutely evenly balanced; in it, the horse goes with clockwork regularity, one diagonal after another, time for time, one hoofbeat matching the other...in the trot, the horse works all his limbs, his shoulders and his hocks to an equal degree; no limb works more than any other, nor different from any other; his muscular development, the strength of thighs and forearm, the flexibility of hocks and knees and indeed of all joints is developed harmoniously.

In brief, no other gait presents so many gymnastic advantages.

Henry Wynmalen *Dressage A Study of the Finer Points of Riding*

However, he expressed, perhaps to a greater extent than many commentators, certain reservations about the trot being the absolute panacea for lack of suppleness. Here, whilst acknowledging the great value of trot, he appears to be querying its role in the context of longitudinal (rather than lateral) suppleness:

Yet the trot fails to some extent in one respect. It has no great effect in suppling the back. Now the whole of the work [previously] discussed, and the methods to be discussed...will all help to correct this stiffness of the back to a greater or smaller degree, but they would frequently not be fully effective if the work were carried out at the trot alone. In dressage the various gaits complement each other and, basic and important though the trot undoubtedly is, we cannot complete our task without the help of the other gaits.

Henry Wynmalen *Dressage A Study of the Finer Points of Riding*

In writing this passage, Wynmalen was, consciously or unconsciously, echoing the thoughts of the great nineteenth century German Master, Gustav Steinbrecht, who stressed the value of correct canter work in longitudinal suppling of the back. However, just like Wynmalen, Steinbrecht took great pains to place the schooling value of each gait in context. At the end of a passage extolling the appropriate use of *canter* in early training, he wrote:

On the other hand, we must qualify the statement that early canter exercises are extremely useful...to be accurate only conditionally. For systematic dressage training the trot offers such great advantages that it will probably always remain its main gait. It not only brings about a degree of activity for the entire body as is necessary for gymnastic work directed towards developing and strengthening all muscles and joints, but it is also not very stressful for the horse and stresses all four legs uniformly.   Gustav Steinbrecht *The Gymnasium of the Horse*

Introducing Trot Work

Before the gaits can have schooling functions – in effect, be exercises of themselves – they must first be developed to a reasonable degree of correctness. If this is not done – if faulty gaits are incorporated into exercises – the inherent defects will adversely affect the exercises, and the quality of the work will be flawed.

In recognition of this, the Masters emphasise the need to establish correct basic trot work. The first step, after preparatory work on the lunge, is the careful introduction of the gait under saddle. One aspect of this care is to avoid being over-demanding:

I have said that five minutes of trotting were enough at first, because it is less the continuance of an exercise than its being properly done that perfects the execution of it.

François Baucher *New Method of Horsemanship* (in *François Baucher, the Man and his Method,* by Hilda Nelson)

At first the horse must be worked at walk and trot only. As when on the longe, every period of trot must be followed by one at the walk to prevent the horse from getting tired; otherwise it would not be possible to preserve the liveliness of the paces and prevent the horse from dragging his feet.

Alois Podhajsky *The Complete Training of Horse and Rider*

Initially only the trot should be used, in a moderate but active tempo, without in any way attempting to artificially position the horse. The pace should be natural, diligent, and in no way collected. To rest the horse, the trot should frequently alternate with the walk...

Gustav Steinbrecht *The Gymnasium of the Horse*

Although Henry Wynmalen wrote the following in the context of lungeing, his emphasis on lack of hindrance would certainly be pertinent to the ridden horse:

First, I desire my horse to deliver the best natural trot, in the best natural attitude whereof he is capable; under my control certainly, but, still more certainly, without any hindrance on my part.

Henry Wynmalen *Dressage A Study of the Finer Points of Riding*

Several of the Masters refer to the first level of trot as the 'natural trot' – the horse re-establishing his natural gait under the weight of the rider, and gaining sufficient strength and confidence so that his back neither sags nor remains in a constant state of tension. This process is explained by Waldemar Seunig:

What is important is that the horse abandons the false tensing or loosening of the back which it exhibited more or less as soon as it was mounted during lungeing. No matter whether the back is tensed or loose...we must always seek to ensure compliance of the back by sitting light in the saddle.

Experience has shown that this objective is best achieved at a natural trot, a gait that the horse chooses itself and at which it is allowed to move with a very loose contact with the bit. The reins must never be allowed to become a crutch, for then the muscles of the back would not abandon their false tension;

they would find support in the rider's hand, and the horse would be spared the trouble of seeking its balance upon its own four legs. Since the rider refuses to provide any support...the horse is compelled to carry itself in natural posture and must, willy-nilly, utilize all the previously tightened muscles for the jobs they have to do in correct locomotion – it must 'uncramp' them.

As soon as this has happened and the horse carries itself without hurrying, the feeling of constraint, which was both cause and effect of a convulsive swinging of the muscles disappears, and our first objective, absence of constraint, has been achieved. As quiet a trot as possible, at which the horse is no longer in

Peter Grunebaum on Mona Lisa; natural trot with loose reins.
From Seunig's Horsemanship.

danger of losing its forward balance and with it its uniform locomotion, its timing, is best suited to these preliminary exercises.

He adds:

In this first stage of training, which may be called the *period of the natural trot* with calm and absence of constraint as its sole interdependent prerequisites, outward form is of no importance whatsoever.   Waldemar Seunig *Horsemanship*

This observation echoes de la Guérinière's strictures that:

These first lessons should have no design in training the mouth or the head: first the horse must become supple and acquire facility in turning easily in both directions...
        François Robichon de la Guérinière *School of Horsemanship*

Seunig continues:

If its gait is naturally long-striding, the horse should not be held back, whereas if the horse is definitely lazy, the riding crop should be used only enough to keep it from holding back.

    As the horse grows somewhat tired – and it will after a few turns around the hall – the last trace of false tension disappears and its timing becomes uniform. The horse supports itself only upon its own legs, has found its natural balance, and therefore moves with natural poise.   Waldemar Seunig *Horsemanship*

The process of achieving the natural trot under saddle is summed up neatly by Wilhelm Müseler:

As soon as the horse has become used to the rider's weight, he will again show his natural paces, which until then will have been somewhat insecure, shorter and hastier. Quiet, regular, long strides are a sign that the first goal has been reached. Influences of the hand could only hinder attainment of this goal. One should be careful not to tire the youngster, nor to overwork him, by too long a trot or by extending the lessons too long.

Wilhelm Müseler *Riding Logic*

Ordinary working trot of young horse.
From Müseler's Riding Logic.

Rising and Sitting Trot

Generally speaking, there is a consensus among the Masters that both rising and sitting trot have legitimate roles in equitation. It may be of interest, however, to begin this section with the individualistic view of James Fillis:

There are two ways of riding at the trot, namely, the French (bumping in the saddle) [sitting trot!] and English (rising in the saddle). The former is of no practical use, although it is an absolutely indispensable school exercise, for giving a good seat to beginners when they trot without stirrups; but I disapprove of it for all other purposes. It is fatiguing to the rider and still more to the horse. I cannot understand why it has been used for such a long time in the army.   James Fillis *Breaking and Riding*

In other words, Fillis saw great value in the sitting trot as an exercise in establishing the rider's seat, but no merit in it otherwise. (Incidentally, the French cannot have taken too much offence at this unflattering description of their sitting trot, since Fillis's name was inscribed on the tablet of *Ecuyers Célèbres* – famous Riding Masters – at Saumur.)

In most cases, the primary concern of the Masters regarding sitting trot is that it should not be employed too early in the horse's training:

Sitting trot should not be used in the first few weeks of working a young horse. We wait until the muscles of his back are stronger.   Reiner Klimke *Basic Training of the Young Horse*

For the young horse it is easier to carry the weight of the rider when he is 'rising at the trot'. The rider should go on doing it until his horse has reached the first stage of balance and when the back muscles are developed.

Richard Wätjen *Dressage Riding*

Furthermore, the process of introducing sitting trot should be a gradual one, requiring discretion and discernment on the rider's part:

It is important, too, when training a green horse, to know how long to do rising trot and when to return to sitting trot, when to have a deep seat and when to elevate the seat. The sitting trot should be done at the moment when the rider feels the horse to be well balanced, free from resistance due to weight displacement. The rider's seat should be deeper when he wishes to push the horse on, and should lighten when he wants the horse to be more passive.

Nuno Oliveira *Notes and Reminiscences of a Portuguese Rider*

During the first stage of training the horse should have been worked in the rising trot. But now that he has been prepared by this work he can gradually be introduced to the sitting trot. To start with, the rider remains sitting very lightly in the saddle for short periods. Particular attention should be paid to preventing the horse from dropping his back and acquiring the habit of going with a hollow back. He must not lie on the reins or change his speed. Nor should he be induced by the change from the rising trot to the sitting trot either to increase or slacken the pace.

If one of these faults creeps in, the rising trot must be resumed and the sitting trot tried only when the trot has become even again. If the young horse is strong enough, he will, in this way, soon become accustomed to the sitting trot. The proof of this will be when he shows no difference in action, impulsion and position whether the rider is sitting or rising. The rider should begin the sitting trot on the large circle and later alternate the exercise by 'going large' around the arena. As a rule the sitting trot will be employed on the circle but an exception can be made at this stage of training. It is an excellent exercise to change from the sitting trot to the rising trot.

In further training the rider will nearly always employ the sitting trot because it offers him a better opportunity to influence his horse and to shape him accordingly; but should the horse, in the course of this work, show any signs of losing impulsion, as may happen with young horses, and show a resistance to going forward, it is then necessary to activate the impulsion by riding forward in a lively rising trot. This will be especially necessary with horses inclined to get behind the bit – a bad habit frequently found in the Lipizzaners.

Alois Podhajsky *The Complete Training of Horse and Rider*

Once the state of unconstraint has been reached, earlier in some horses and later in others, there is no reason not to assume the soft, elastic normal seat. The time for this has come when the back neither arches nor sags in a cramp and thus is active to a certain extent though not yet compliant in the equestrian sense.

The author gives a caveat to this in a footnote:

If the rider does not have a really soft and supple seat, it is better to use the sitting trot only after the horse's contact with the bit is assured, and the elastically swinging active back invites one to sit down…A sitting trot at too early a stage disturbs the movements and back activity of the horse and communicates its roughness to the reins, so that the freedom and extension of the horse's strides suffer and the horse is 'held up', so to speak, by the impact of the rider's weight.

Waldemar Seunig Horsemanship

In The Essence of Horsemanship, Seunig discusses further the process of taking sitting trot:

The rider remains in rising trot until the horse's back starts to oscillate. Now, gently, the rider starts to sit the trot and, glued to the saddle, follows its movement back and forth as he lets himself be drawn ever further down. The rider continually tests the independence of his seat and the self-carriage of the horse by running his hands up the horse's neck.

Waldemar Seunig The Essence of Horsemanship

Henry Wynmalen, Master of Foxhounds and practitioner of High School dressage, took a pragmatic overview of the two forms of trot:

The rider may trot either rising…or sitting…Both methods have their uses. It is not possible, nor necessary, to lay down hard and fast rules regarding the use of either…during our work of training the horse.

Generally, the rider will use the rising trot for all ordinary work in the open country…Outside, on uneven ground, the rising trot is more comfortable, less tiring and therefore better for both horse and rider. On perfectly level going, in the school and elsewhere, the sitting trot may be equally comfortable for the rider, and therefore also for the horse, even at the most energetic and extended paces. But it will never be comfortable at any strong trot until the horse's back really swings and carries its rider as if on springs. There is no advantage to be gained, either from the rider's or the horse's point of view, by insisting on a seat which is uncomfortable to both...So, when we are schooling our horse, it is sensible to take the rising trot whenever the sitting trot tends to discomfort...

However, while he warns against using sitting trot thoughtlessly, or too early, he is quick to point out the advantages of its correct use:

The sitting trot unites the rider more closely to his horse; rider and horse feel each other more intimately; consequently the aids gain in delicacy and precision; the rider is much more conscious of rhythm, of swing and of cadence and is able to work intelligently for their development; in fact, the sitting trot is a sensitive and accurate barometer of the degree of suppleness achieved in his horse's back; his comfort will increase *pro rata* of the progress made in that direction...

Henry Wynmalen *Dressage A Study of the Finer Points of Riding*

The Rider's Seat and Posture

Before explaining the correct method of rising at the trot, two Masters echo Wynmalen's warning against the incorrect use of sitting trot:

Must we pass our existence at a sitting trot, kicking the animal with our legs, tiring ourselves, and tiring the back of the poor animal? Is it by trotting for hours with the horse's head at liberty that impulsion will be given to the horse? Neither one, nor the other; it is only necessary to know how to vary the cadence of the trot and to know how to rise to the trot. It may seem strange that I say it is important to learn how to trot rising, as so many riders think that after the first lessons they know how to do this very well. Rising trot is not limited to knowing how to lift oneself off the saddle and fall back in rhythm and cadence. It is necessary for the rider to know how to use the legs without effort or tenseness in order to push the horse forward while rising in the saddle.

It is vital that while rising to the trot the upper torso of the rider be not too far forward, and that it be kept at a constant degree of inclination. When the rider comes down into the saddle, the legs should greet the horse's body, embracing it in a forward movement.   Nuno Oliveira *Reflections on Equestrian Art*

One of the main causes of improper tension of the [**horse's**] back muscles, is the rider with a rigidly straight back. There can be nothing more painful and fatiguing for the horse than the sitting trot without stirrups when the rider is forced to maintain a smart military posture, with an exaggeratedly straight back; this exercise used to be described in the German (and French) cavalry as 'pepper pounding'. With a young horse, when he sits to the trot, the rider ought to sit on the buttocks, leaning forward from the waist (not the hip joint), so that the pelvis can be tilted very slightly backward and move in the direction of the movement, towards the pommel of the saddle. However, with all young horses, the beginning of every lesson must be either at the rising trot or at the canter with the buttocks clear of the saddle.

Üdo Burger *The Way to Perfect Horsemanship*

Both these extracts, especially that of Burger, strike a chord with Fillis's dislike of the sitting trot. Perhaps it was this 'pepper pounding' that he had in mind when he described the

French sitting trot as 'bumping in the saddle'. Fillis's explanation of how to rise to the trot is as follows:

When we rise to the trot there are neither jerks nor reactions. The rider should have his loins slightly bent, and consequently the upper part of his body should be inclined a little forward. He should not try by rising to follow or to anticipate the movements of the horse, but should let himself be raised. His ankle joints and knees acting together will sustain his movement, and will make him descend softly into the saddle, and into the cadence marked by the pace of the horse. He should always rise from *under* himself, that is to say, he should let the horse raise him, while helping the movement with the knee and ankle joints; but the upper part of the body should do nothing. Otherwise, the muscles of the loins and shoulders will be contracted, the rider will become stiff, and will not be firmly united to his horse. The body ought to rise and fall as a whole.

The rider who hollows his back, in place of using only his legs, necessarily carries his abdomen forward when he rises, and backward when he descends into the saddle, than which nothing can be more ungraceful.

Only one-third (the ball) of the foot should be placed in the stirrup. If the foot is 'home', the ankle will lose all its elasticity and consequently the trot will become stiff and painful.

James Fillis *Breaking and Riding*

Further descriptions of posture for rising trot are given by Richard Wätjen...

...For the rising trot the rider...rises from the saddle at each alternate stride. He should keep his knees flat on the saddle without pressing and put his weight down on the stirrups with ankles and heels well down. Under no circumstances should he permit the lower part of the leg to go in front of the vertical; in coming down in the saddle he must keep his legs slightly behind it.

The rider should carry the upper part of the body somewhat forward, thus following the movement of the horse...

The rider soon gets the feel for the proper diagonal and the smooth change, but he must be taught the correct method of rising at the trot in order to use the driving and restraining aids in a proper way, thus improving his horse's balance.

Richard Wätjen *Dressage Riding*

...Waldemar Seunig:

A few words concerning...the rising trot: every time the rider slips back into the saddle, he should pay special attention to pulling his base of support forward and to his driving leg, because the buttocks, which are continuously in the saddle at the sitting trot, transmitting the driving action of the small of the back to the horse, are fully in the saddle only at every second step at the rising trot. Buttocks that are pushed out at the rear and a rise at the trot that is higher than that required by the impulse of motion destroy impulsion...

It cannot be repeated too often that the rider's knee and ankle joints must be supple at the rising trot. If they are stiff, they make it harder for the legs to lie close to the horse's body, and imperil a precise gradation of their action as well as the firmness of the seat, which will then seek support in the stirrups even when the normal seat is used. Every rider can readily convince himself that pressing the heels down hard during posting also contributes largely to keeping the rider's base of support close to the saddle.　　　　Waldemar Seunig *Horsemanship*

...and Erik Herbermann:

- We have a mobile, dynamic centre of balance which moves between the foot and the knee.
- We must have a well-stretched position, and freedom and independent balance of the upper body.
- The inclination of the upper body should be *slightly* tilted forward; the angle is directly related to the centre of balance of the horse. If the horse is tense and rushing on the forehand, the upper body should be brought forward slightly to coincide with the horse's centre of balance; only then can the horse's rhythm and balance be restored through either half-halting or driving. Once the horse is in balance, and allows itself to be driven, then the upper body can come somewhat closer to the vertical again.
- The horse should move the rider (a trampoline effect); it shouldn't be necessary to stand up forcibly.
- The motion of the seat should be forward and back, the hips moving through the elbows; as opposed to an exaggerated up and down, jack-in-the-box attitude. The rise should be as small as possible.
- The lower back should be steady, neither hollow while rising, nor round while sitting. The correct steadiness of the spine* can best be achieved when the hip joints are truly relaxed and loose. [*Author's footnote describes this steadiness thus: Where the rider's torso, made up of the body and hip, remains as a unit. The wobbly, loose, 'doughy' lower back is to be avoided.]
- Be well relaxed and 'let down' – sit and rise honestly. A non-sitting, hovering over the saddle is ineffective. However, do not drop harshly onto the horse's back when sitting.
- Care must be taken to rise and sit squarely, to avoid a twisting or mincing motion of either the hips or the shoulders.

- The knee and lower leg must be steady. The knee acts as a pivot.
- The weight should go clearly into the relaxed ankles at each stride, the heels showing a slight dip each time the rider rises.
- Relative to the horse's mouth, the hands are to be *absolutely motionless,* without exception! This, however, does not mean rigid.   Erik Herbermann *Dressage Formula*

(Herbermann's point about diagonals is included in the following section of this book.)

The care with which these writers describe the rising trot hints at the fact that it is only beneficial if carried out correctly. This point is emphasised by Charles Harris, who states plainly that:

The rising trot is physically less demanding for the rider – and the horse – when carried out correctly. Carried out badly, it is the cause of many back injuries, and tends to hollow the horse's back.   Charles Harris *Fundamentals of Riding*

...before providing a summary of correct posture for both sitting and rising trot:

Correct sitting trot posture
The rider's body is held vertical without any stiffness whatsoever, with the loins, seat, and thighs absorbing the up/down/forward action of the horse in trot.

To the onlooker, it should appear that the rider is simply sitting still.

Correct rising trot posture
The rider's body is held vertical or just in front of the vertical, not exceeding 2 to 3 degrees. The actual 'rising' from the saddle

The compression spring action of the lumbar vertebrae is to keep the back slightly braced and body upright

The 'rise/ease' of the rear part of the seat is minimal with the whole of the crutch area remaining on the saddle. The upper part of the body should not be thrown upward and forward lifting the rider completely off the saddle seat

Buttocks/thighs/ankles act as compression coiled springs

Rising trot—buttocks/thighs act as a coiled spring

In sitting trot the main absorbing compression spring is the buttocks, aided by the action of the braced back which can elevate and lighten the seat without losing the full contact with the saddle. If the action of the horse is stiff and jerky the rider can then use the thighs by gently closing them from the top downward, which tends to lighten/ease the seat on the saddle

Primary absorbing compression springs—lumbar vertebrae and buttocks

Secondary absorbing compression spring—if needed—thighs

Ankles should be a last resort if the weight has to be eased from saddle

Sitting trot—loins/buttocks/thighs act as coiled compression springs in combinations to suit trot variants

Rider's posture for rising and sitting trot, from Charles Harris's Fundamentals of Riding.

is minimal, and is achieved by allowing the horse's action to slightly ease the rider's weight from the rear of the buttocks, and not lifting the whole seat from the saddle resulting from standing up in the stirrups. To sum-up, the crutch does not move from the saddle, and the rider simply half-eases the rear of his buttocks from the rear of the saddle. There should never be any daylight between the rider's seat and the saddle.

Charles Harris *Fundamentals of Riding*

Diagonals in Trot

As commandant of the Ecole de Cavalerie at Saumur, General Alexis-François L'Hotte spent a good deal of time trying to convince high-ranking officers of the benefits of rising trot. It is hardly surprising, therefore, that in his book, *Questions Équestres,* he analyses the movement in minute detail. Certain aspects of his analysis may suggest that cavalrymen of his era performed the movement in a somewhat more extravagant fashion then would be considered 'correct' nowadays. As a result of his studies, he observed that the diagonal with which the rider rises gains more ground than the other diagonal – a fact that can certainly contribute to the horse's crookedness but which can also be used to alleviate it. Here is an extract from his extensive text on the subject:

The displacement of the torso which involves the rising trot, although kept within limits, also exerts on the horse an action that is rather sensitive, so that the diagonal, with which the rider moves in concert, covers more ground than the other one. Every rider who has practised the rising trot with some attention, has certainly been convinced of this fact.

Here is the explanation:

Let us suppose that the rider, trotting with the right diagonal, has just received the relaxation of this diagonal and yields to it. When the inclination forward of the rider's torso reaches its limit, and he supports himself on the irons, that is the moment when the whole effect of the relaxation of the left diagonal occurs, which moves and pushes forward the right diagonal which is, at the moment, supportive. The latter now gains much more ground than the weight of the rider, now totally brought forward, solicited.

When, in turn, the right diagonal comes down, it is the moment when the rider...lets himself go backwards. The weight of his torso, carried closer to the haunches, annuls the effect produced by the relaxation of the right diagonal and, therefore, restricts the extent of the ground that the left diagonal covers and is, at the moment, supportive...

The diagonal with which the rider trots gains more ground than does the other one, and results in the haunches being pulled to that side and, as a consequence, making them deviate to the right if the rider is in accord with the right diagonal.

The effect is appreciable with all horses, but especially with those who, through dressage, have acquired a rigorously straight position. A single hack...trotting constantly on the same diagonal will suffice to affect the horse's straight position. This will be noticeable the next day when the horse is ridden in the *manège* at the beginning of the working period.

With certain horses whose straight position has been strengthened, there are some who are so affected by the displacements of the rider's torso, that, already after the first stride, the haunches deviate either to the right or to the left when the rider alternates from one diagonal to the other.

One must thus trot with both diagonals if one wishes to

prevent the straight position of the horse from being affected, and to equalize the work of his limbs.

Seldom is the horse who has not yet been developed through schooling, and who has been trotted indiscriminately with one or the other diagonal, able to trot with equal ease. A preference for one or the other diagonal finds its source in certain imperfections of the horse's structure, nature having apparently neglected one part of its work. Then, too, it may be the result of a false position acquired through habit.

With the horse who shows a marked deviation from the straight position, the rising trot is always taken as easily with the diagonal on the side where the horse traverses, as taken with difficulty with the opposite diagonal. In this case, one sees horses lose all the brilliance of their actions, expressing difficulties and confusion in their movement. There are even those who...actually change their step, so that the solicitations exerted by the rider's body, rather than opposing the traversed position, go along with it.

It is also to be noted that, either by habit or due to an irregularity in their position, a number of riders have a marked predisposition of always trotting on the same diagonal, and have great difficulty going from the customary one to the other...To have no preference for a diagonal says something favourable as much for the rider as for the horse...

Both the horse and rider, but, perhaps more so the horse, benefited from the rising trot in that he no longer had to receive those chocks with which his dorsal column, set in motion, had to cope with at each stride...The rider, too, by trotting this way, finds resources with which to straighten the horse who traverses, regularize his gait, and obtain the canter on the lead the horse has refused to take. To achieve this latter result, the rider must trot with the lead which the horse cannot take and progressively lengthen the gait. When the horse ...can no longer sustain this gait, he will be forced to take, of his own accord, the canter on the side he traverses, striking off on the lead that gains the most ground and which is the one with which the rider trots.

Alexis-François L'Hotte *Questions Équestres*

James Fillis, a contemporary of L'Hotte, does not appear to have made the same observation about the differing stride length of the diagonals in rising trot. He states that:

The natural trot of a horse which is not upset or suffering, is an alternate and absolutely identical movement of the two diagonals.   James Fillis *Breaking and Riding*

Although, since he uses the phrase 'natural trot', it is not absolutely clear whether he is referring to the horse at liberty or under saddle. However, his remarks regarding the rider's propensity for a particular diagonal are certainly much in accord with the points raised by L'Hotte:

At the rising trot, the rider can trot either on the left or the right diagonal biped...The rider is said to trot on the left diagonal biped, when he rises at the same moment that the horse raises his left fore foot, and comes down on the saddle, when the horse puts that foot to the ground...

The rider ought to be able to ride at the trot equally well on one biped, as on the other biped, and should be able to change from one to the other, so as to relieve himself, and especially the horse, during a long journey, but this requires a certain amount of practice to do. A rider ought to learn how to know on what biped he is, which is difficult at first...

It is worthy of note that each rider naturally adopts one particular biped, and almost always without knowing that he does so, and he becomes so habituated to it that he feels ill at ease when he changes to the other biped.

James Fillis *Breaking and Riding*

L'Hotte died in 1904, the year in which another Master of the French School, General Decarpentry, joined the Cadre Noir. As a consequence of his background, Decarpentry was much influenced by the teachings of L'Hotte and Baucher, but he also studied the works of many other Masters with great zeal. In his book *Academic Equitation,* he reiterates L'Hotte's observation that, in rising trot, the diagonal on which the rider rises covers more ground than the other, and develops the subject of hind leg deviation:

The rising trot procures...other...advantages as it allows the rider to influence in different ways the alternating movements of the diagonals in order to achieve perfect symmetry of their development. The different attitudes of the upper body when the seat rises or descends cause displacements of weight which affect each pair of legs, and therefore the movement of one pair is developed under conditions of equilibrium different from those under which the opposite number works; it can be observed that the diagonal upon which one trots usually covers more ground than the other, and that its hind leg tends to step in the tracks of the fore-leg, thus to deviate to this side of the diagonal, causing the croup itself to move to the same side.

In a footnote he adds:

This is only true in the long run. If one starts trotting on the left diagonal on a horse which is used to being trotted on the right one only, he will certainly not develop immediately the range of his left diagonal. On the contrary, he will be surprised and upset, and will use it even less than usual and often attempt to throw his rider back onto the right diagonal by putting in false beats…It is only by persevering, sometimes for very long, with the trot on the left diagonal that one overcomes the horse's resistance and gradually gets him to use this diagonal as willingly as the right one…   General Decarpentry *Academic Equitation*

Over half a century after L'Hotte expressed his views about riders always rising on the same diagonal, Henry Wynmalen, who observed many riders both in the school and across country, was still concerned that many used rising trot ignorantly, thinking more of their own comfort than their effect upon the horse:

Unfortunately, it is my experience that an astonishing number of riders…are quite ignorant of the simple principles involved.

In the first place…we avoid, by using the rising trot, one bump in two. We come down in the saddle as one particular diagonal pair of legs meet the ground and rise from the saddle as the same pair leave the ground. We miss the impact of the other diagonal pair of legs altogether. We may rise either on the near fore-off hind diagonal or on the off fore-near hind diagonal. The fact which astonishes me is that any number of riders are in the habit of always rising on the same diagonal. They appear oblivious to the fact that one can and should rise on both diagonals alternately; in the sense that we trot away for the first ten minutes or so, we use, say, the right diagonal…and that during the next period of trotting we use the left diagonal…and so on…If we fail to do so we tire our horse, and in the end wear him out, one-sidedly. We also disturb the perfect even rhythm of the gait in the long run, render our horse one-sided and tend to ruin his straightness. In that respect, the experienced horseman may at times be able to use the rising trot on one particular diagonal rather than the other, temporarily, to improve unevenness in his horse's gait.

Henry Wynmalen *Dressage A Study of the Finer Points of Riding*

The topics of straightening crookedness and strengthening weakness are taken up by John Winnett:

To trot, a horse associates his legs by diagonal pairs. The diagonal takes on the name of the foreleg; right diagonal signifying right foreleg and left hind. A diagonal is supported when its legs are on the ground and is suspended when its legs are in the air. A rider trots on the right diagonal when his or her buttocks contact the saddle as the right foreleg touches the ground. The weak diagonal is always the one which feels more uncomfortable to sit on. There is, therefore, an incentive to rise more on the weak diagonal to make it stronger...

A good simple method to make a young horse straight, is to change diagonals at the rising trot every four, three and two strides in sequence. This is especially efficacious cross-country. The exercise builds up the weak diagonal and develops cadence in the early stages of training. A horse who is constantly trotted on the same diagonal will tend to canter on the same lead. He will become crooked and will use himself much more on one side than the other.

John Winnett *Dressage as Art in Competition*

While Waldemar Seunig picks up on the connection between trot and diagonals and the canter lead, and echoes the point made by L'Hotte:

To assure that the horse will break into the correct canter lead, the rider must for the time being and against all normal rules rise when the inside front leg and the outside hind leg [diagonal] comes to the ground. This is the only time when rising on this diagonal is permitted.

Waldemar Seunig *The Essence of Horsemanship*

Judging from the final sentence of this extract, Seunig had, by the time he wrote this book (1961), somewhat modified the theories propounded in his earlier work, *Horsemanship*. Indeed, in the preface to the third edition of *Horsemanship (1956)* he wrote 'They say, "The rider's education is never finished", and I have had many opportunities to increase my own experience with horses...ever since the first edition appeared in 1943.' Leonard Mins, translator of *Horsemanship,* wrote of the author dealing with 'every possible shade of meaning...'. The following extract, which certainly shows a desire for detailed analysis, makes reference to the debate about which diagonal to ride upon:

And now for [the] much disputed question: *On which hind leg should the rider post?*

The only answer that can be given here is quite a general one. Special cases, such as weakness of individual legs or the refractoriness of ruined horses, must be left to the tact and feeling of the rider in question.

The following is recommended in the riding hall for working a raw remount or a horse that is not responsive enough, is ignorant of the restraining leg control, or does not fully accept it: rising on the outside hind leg. This leg, which carries the heavier load, will advance in the direction of the plumb line through the centre of gravity in accordance with the horse's instinctive effort to find its lateral balance (unless it is disturbed by a rider who provokes crookedness)...That is why the expedient of departing, say, at the gallop right from the trot, when the horse is trotting on the first (outside) hind foot, almost always succeeds without previous 'positioning' with equestrian longitudinal flexion (which the horse in question could not assume). Owing to its load this leg will find the position appropriate to the future outside hind leg at the gallop more readily than its unburdened partner. Another reason for preferring the burden placed on the outside hind leg when the young horse is worked at the rising trot in the riding hall is that this spares the inside hind leg, which does more of the work on the unavoidable curved lines anyhow. With the trained horse, which trots on the inside hind leg in the riding hall, as we shall see, the bending gymnastics to which this leg is subjected deliberately on curved tracks are reinforced by this method of loading...

The following is our reply to the question of which hind leg we should post on in the highly advanced horse, which can already move 'in position' and whose lateral responsiveness has consequently been so far developed that it can be ridden in circles no more than six steps in diameter without losing its impulsion...in the riding hall it should be on the inside hind leg. The reason for this is that the rider's seat, adapted to the longitudinal flexion of the horse on the curved lines that frequently occur in the riding hall, which also include close turns, provides the natural position for the inner leg just behind the girth.

Following the natural rhythm of motion of the rising trot on the inside hind leg, the rider's inner leg swings from the position that is best for driving when the inner hind leg has entered its phase of support after advancing...This control, which makes the grounded inner hind leg, the supporting leg, thrust away from the ground with increased force, stimulates the outer hind leg to reach forward vigorously in its swinging phase in order to provide room for the stronger thrust of the inner hind leg.

This greater engagement of the outer hind leg is necessary because...it has to travel a longer distance than the inner hind leg

on the stretched side of the horse's body and the outer edge of
the curved track…The rider's outside leg, with its natural position further behind the girth, acts in a supporting role, for the
inside hind leg (which it would have to drive forward in time
with the swings of the horse's body) requires less forward drive.
It has to travel a shorter distance on the concave side of the
horse's body despite the heavier load placed upon it in the turns.

**When trotting small circles, even though using their legs to
support the horse as described, most riders would normally sit
to the trot. They might wonder why Seunig talks about rising
trot in this context. He goes on to give a rationale:**

Summing up, the rising trot on the inside leg achieves two objec-
tives on curved tracks: first, the flexing gymnastics of the inside
hind leg are deliberately aided. Second, the job of the outside
hind leg, which has to travel the greater distance, is made much
easier by relieving it of some of its load and by the leg control
that is applied at the correct moment when the rider sits down
on the inside hind leg, thus assisting in the further reach and
engagement of the outside hind leg.

On trotting in the open, Seunig is more succinct:

In working in the open with healthy, harmoniously built horses
the hind leg should be changed every time the horse takes off in
trot in order to strengthen and supple the muscles, ligaments and
joints on both sides of the body, and thus prevent the horse from
becoming crooked.

**In adding the following, the author, who was Chief Riding
Master of the Yugoslavian Cavalry School, seems to be making
a distinction between general practice when riding outside, and**

the demands of very strenuous work, when a tired or unsound horse might be trying to 'save' a leg:

On long rides – cross-country and marches – use the rising trot on the hind leg 'offered' to us by the horse. Pedantic dressage and constraint would be a waste of energy that might be costly later on. In general avoid burdening a diagonal pair of legs if one of the legs needs to be spared.   Waldemar Seunig *Horsemanship*

On the topic of riding on a specific diagonal, succinct rationales are provided by Richard Wätjen:

...While on the right rein, the rider sits in the saddle when the off hindleg and near foreleg, called the left diagonal, come to the ground, and on the left rein when the near hindleg and off foreleg, called the right diagonal, come to the ground. The reason for coming down in the saddle on the inside hindleg is to achieve an increased and energetic engagement of the inside hock by the driving aids of the rider, especially in cornering and circling. When changing rein the rider must change the diagonal without interrupting the cadence...

There are exceptional occasions when one uses the other diagonal for a special reason; for instance, on the left rein one can use the left diagonal in order to influence the off hindleg more, but one should never continue using the same diagonal on both reins.

It is most important to train the young horse equally on both diagonals and to change frequently...when hacking, otherwise the horse becomes stiff and one-sided, with the result that the horse strikes off easier with one foreleg leading than the other.

Richard Wätjen *Dressage Riding*

...and Erik Herbermann:

Rise as the horse's outside front leg goes forward and, in order to exercise both sides of the horse equally, remember the need to switch diagonals when changing the rein.* Sitting as the inside hind leg bears weight will also assist in animating the horse. [*Author's footnote: During training it can be helpful to change diagonals, back and forth, independent of changing the rein. This can help to encourage the horse to use both hind legs evenly.]

Erik Herbermann *Dressage Formula*

Sitting when the outside foreleg comes back, and rising as it goes forward, amounts to riding on the same diagonal. These two authors are describing the same movement in different terms, a point made succinctly by Alois Podhajsky:

In this stage the *rising trot* should be employed and the rider should ride on the outside diagonal, that is to say, he should rise…when the inside hind leg and the outside foreleg come off the ground and return to the saddle when the same diagonal returns to the ground.

Alois Podhajsky *The Complete Training of Horse and Rider*

As the previous extract from *Dressage A Study of the Finer Points of Riding* shows, Henry Wynmalen shared the general view that favouring one particular diagonal would affect straightness and influence crookedness in the long term. However, he was less convinced of the need to ride specifically on the inside or outside diagonal of the moment. The following extract also highlights the point that, formerly, many dressage tests either allowed or demanded periods of rising trot:

The dressage rider has to meet certain requirements expected of him in the arena with respect to the rising trot. This concerns the method of going round bends and corners, whether to rise on the outside diagonal or the inside one. The majority hold that it is preferable to rise on the outside diagonal. Others hold the opposite view. Neither side has ever been able to offer convincing argument. It is more a matter of 'feel'. My feeling is with…the majority, but I am quite ready to admit that there may be nothing much in it. However, I make my practice accordingly. There is no rule about it, except that each competitor, free to choose his own system, must be consistent. In other words, once a competitor has ridden one bend on either the inside or the outside diagonal, he has to continue the same system; so, in changing from one bend to another at the rising trot, he must change the diagonal or be faulted.

Henry Wynmalen *Dressage A Study of the Finer Points of Riding*

Perhaps the final word on this topic should go to Waldemar Seunig, who once said: 'In the art of riding, nothing is invariably right or invariably wrong'.

Working Trot

The working trot – the basic form of the gait that can fulfil schooling functions – is established out of the natural trot.

Young horse in balance in a working trot. Reiner Klimke on Volt. From Klimke's Basic Training of the Young Horse.

The working trot is the same as the natural trot except that one asks for a little more freshness to the movement, a little more animation and engagement of the hind quarters than would be natural. Through sympathetic aids the horse is encouraged to work...

We ... take care not to practise the medium trot too early...To begin with it is enough to increase the freshness of the strides from a natural to a working trot.

Reiner Klimke Basic Training of the Young Horse

The *working trot* is the principal gait employed in subsequent gymnastic training of the young horse, as the natural trot has been up to now, because it compels the muscles to be appropriately active without over-exerting them. Since the trotting horse has only two legs grounded at one time, and these legs are grounded for a shorter period than at the walk, say, it is harder for the horse to use them in resisting the rider's influences. Nor is it easier for the horse to hold back arbitrarily, because the inherent thrust of the trot, which is increasingly associated with impulsion, makes it hard to do so.

Waldemar Seunig Horsemanship

Commenting on attempts to define the working trot in terms of competition rules, Dr H.L.M. van Schaik charts a history of FEI definitions of the trot variants as they vacillate between German, French and English, remarking wryly that:

All the misconceptions and fallacies surrounding the working trot are proof that it is one thing to translate a foreign term literally and quite another thing to understand its meaning.

Dr H.L.M. van Schaik *Misconceptions and Simple Truths in Dressage*

He goes on to make the observations that:

Since the working trot is a schooling movement, it cannot really be covered by a definition. It has to be made clear to the riders what the purpose of this schooling is; namely, to activate the hindquarters and to get the horse steadily on the bit. This is a process in which the horse learns to trot in a steady, balanced way...

...It indeed is called a working trot, because the horse has to work in order to be able to execute a rhythmic, balanced trot, using all his muscles, so that he finally will be able not only to perform the trot as normally used in road work, but also that he can be schooled in the whole scale of the different trots. Working trot is in the first place a schooling gait.

Dr H.L.M. van Schaik *Misconceptions and Simple Truths in Dressage*

Waldemar Seunig shares the view that there is no point in attempting to define working trot in terms of specific speed or frequency:

There is no definite rate for the working trot...for different horses have strides of different length.

Waldemar Seunig *Horsemanship*

Of course, definition and description are different matters. Richard Wätjen describes the working trot in very simple terms:

The rider should choose the pace at which his mount can be easily kept in balance in a cadenced trot in order to achieve a proper sequence of the steps; he keeps a light contact with the

Richard Wätjen, ordinary working trot. From Wätjen's
Dressage Riding.

reins. The head and neck carriage and the pace should depend
on the stage of training the horse has reached.

Richard Wätjen *Dressage Riding*

Other writers go into greater detail:

It is at the working trot that we first teach the horse to carry
itself. The working trot is rarely the normal trot of a horse;

it is developed from the normal trot on the lightest possible contact which is used during the period of breaking-in to accustom the horse to the presence of the rider. The working trot has a determined rhythm which should be known by the rider; since the natural trot of the horse is usually too slow, too hurried, or irregular. To obtain the working trot the rider has to regulate the movement with either hands or legs and the rein tension must become more positive than mere contact. The rider must get the horse to work energetically at a regular rhythm and a steady but brisk speed, picking up its feet, flexing and extending smoothly and equally all the joints of the hindquarters. It must eventually learn to obtain the speed of its own accord. The movements of its limbs must gradually become rounder, more expansive and its trot easier to sit on.

Most importantly, the weight has to be distributed equally over all four legs; each leg must be equally loaded, so that none wears out sooner than the others. The hind legs must therefore be made to engage, that is to advance sufficiently to relieve the forelegs of an excess of weight, but greater engagement of hocks, pronounced flexion of haunches, lightness of the forehand, elevation of head and neck must not be demanded; they belong to a much later stage of schooling.

Alfred Knopfhart *Fundamentals of Dressage*

John Winnett suggests a method by which the rider can establish the rhythm of the working trot for an individual horse:

It is important to find and establish the proper rhythm and tempo of the horse's working trot. To do this, the rider must drive the horse forward until he starts to shorten the length of his stride. This is the threshold; the point where the tempo is too fast, and the horse shortens his stride and runs forward. When you reach this threshold, back the tempo down a fraction and you will have the working trot for that particular horse. Other than to establish this threshold it is very bad practice to ride the horse forward to the point where he loses his length of stride, since this results in loss of rhythm, and eventually total loss of pure gait.

Winnett's caveat in the last sentence is reinforced by an earlier passage on lungeing the young horse, where the author writes:

It would be a grave mistake to drive the horse forward in a tempo beyond his physical suppleness and strength, for doing so would ruin the true rhythm of the trot. It would also be a mistake to let the horse lag behind the bit; the trainer must, therefore, create and maintain the proper tempo and rhythm.

John Winnett *Dressage as Art in Competition*

Reiner Klimke, with whom Winnett studied, also comments on the rider's role in establishing correct rhythm, and warns against hurrying the horse:

To maintain the natural sequence, in other words the correct rhythm of the pace (regularity) and with a constant repetition (even tempo), is what is called in German '*takt*'. To regulate this is the most important duty of the rider of the young horse. This is achieved thorough the rider's smooth adaptation of the movement to help the horse find its balance...

The way the rider gets his horse balanced is very important. In the beginning he should concentrate on '*losgelassenheit*' [**removal of tension**] and establish rhythm, then use careful aids to help the hind quarters come under the horse to achieve better balance. If the rider asks too much, too early, the pace will simply speed up...

Reiner Klimke *Basic Training of the Young Horse*

The transitional process from natural trot to working trot is described in detail by Waldemar Seunig. The starting point is that:

The young horse must already have reached a state of confidence and be familiar with the natural, regular trot. This means that, after it has worked off its initial tenseness, it should trot along unrestrained, without either rushing or being behind the bit, with natural self-carriage on very light rein contact on a straight line.   Waldemar Seunig *The Essence of Horsemanship*

Waldemar Seunig's own drawing of correct working trot, from
The Essence of Horsemanship.

As a result of too high carriage and false collection, the hind legs leave the ground too late. The uncollected horse moves with stiff quarters trailing out behind. The co-ordination between hindquarters and forehand is interrupted (there is a curve in the vertical line of the back), and the horse, not evenly on the bit, is a so-called 'stiff mover'.

(Above and opposite) Seunig's own drawings of incorrect working trot, with his captions, from The Essence of Horsemanship.

The transition to working trot must be carried out with care:

The *transitions* from the natural trot, which is always employed at the beginning of the lesson until unconstrained movement is achieved, to the working rate must be made gradually, with increasing controls that are adapted to the sensitivity of the

Working trot
The diagonal hoof beats are regular, but are dull and dragging.
Lack of impulsion and forward reaching of the hind legs, weak
hindquarters, poorly connected to rest of body. This should be
corrected by a lighter rider, through using a more driving and forward seat, setting the horse's head and neck carriage lower.

horse. If this involves loss of timing, mere increase in speed is
valueless, and damages the progress of dressage. In this work one
should always remember that raising the natural trot to the
working trot must be achieved by lengthening the stride of the
hind legs, which thrust off more powerfully and engage farther
forward, the number of strides remaining the same [i.e. per given
period] Waldemar Seunig *Horsemanship*

In the same work, Seunig develops this theme:

After a few weeks the muscles, principally those of the hindquarters, the back, and the neck, will be so strengthened by the natural trot, which forces them to be active without overexertion, that the rider can increase the demands he makes upon the horse. The muscles of the hindquarters and those of the back coupled to them have had no occasion to pulsate vigorously...owing to the slight energy developed in the hindquarters up to now. All that we have done has been to restore the same freedom and sureness to the gait that the horse possessed when it moved about easily in the pasture...

Though this kind of locomotion is the natural one for the horse in freedom, this mere absence of constraint hardly satisfies the requirements of riding. The rider would be unable to lengthen the stride...to the limits of the mechanism provided by the horse's conformation, thus making full use of its machinery.

Nor would he be able to prevent premature wearing out of the horse, because only when the hind legs develop energetic thrust and engage far forward – an additional effort that the horse makes only when induced to do so by the external driving controls – do the muscles of the back swing with the energy required for relieving the legs.

Active, driving influences must compel the horse that now saunters along wholly unconstrained...to make full use of its muscles, which are now freely extended but working at only half their power. They must make it come up to the controls, especially the hands, and become supple.

Waldemar Seunig *Horsemanship*

Col. Mylius on Cottstown; working trot with acquired poise.
From Seunig's Horsemanship.

A prerequisite for these driving aids being effective is that:

The horse must allow himself to be 'driven'. Therefore he must already understand and respond to the driving aids so that he maintains the tempo as determined by the effect of the seat and the regulating hands, neither rushing nor becoming cramped. The gait shall, with a relaxed back and even contact, be lively and rhythmic, in other words, pure.

Also, in…

…responding to the driving aids – the increased thrust of the hindquarters – the horse should move forward in regular and increasingly longer strides, coming onto the bit. Through forward, downward extended neck and a marked oscillation of the back, the contact becomes more definite. The neck is stabilized in front of the withers. Preparation has now commenced for the other movements at the trot.

Waldemar Seunig   The Essence of Horsemanship

Many of the points made by Seunig are echoed by Wilhelm Müseler, who emphasises the role of unconstrained forward movement in alleviating crookedness, and makes the point that the rider's hands must *allow*, not *compel* the horse to start seeking the bit.

From then on, all further work consists of riding the horse well forward at a quiet working trot. The pace should be just a trifle faster than…the horse offers voluntarily to go. As soon as he shows any inclination to get shorter and slacker in his stride, the swing and liveliness of his pace will be lost. By urging him on and forward the rider begins to impose his will upon the horse; it must be the rider who determines the pace and not the horse. This is the beginning of all putting to the aids. The free forward movement must not be impaired by the rider's hands trying to shape the horse at the same time, because shape or form are not what counts here. All tensions and all one-sidedness which become apparent, as well as all short or nappy strides must, so to say, be ridden out forward, in a quiet, striding trot. The horse will thereby quite naturally drop his head and neck – provided the rider does not work against it with his hands – and he will on his own initiative try to find a steady support on the bit.

Wilhelm Müseler   Riding Logic

*Felix Bürkner on Bober, ordinary working trot with loose back.
From Müseler's* Riding Logic.

Developing the Working Trot

The horse that makes fifty steps at a trot regularly is much further advanced in his education than if he made a thousand in a bad position.

François Baucher *New Method of Horsemanship* (in *François Baucher, the Man and his Method*, by Hilda Nelson)

The same author describes the requirements for, and the benefits of a balanced, united trot:

The condition indispensable to a good trot is perfect equilibrium of the body. Equilibrium which keeps up a regular movement of the diagonal fore and hind feet, gives them an equal elevation and extension, with such lightness that the horse can easily execute all changes of direction, moderate his speed, halt or increase his speed without effort. The foreparts have not, then, the appearance of towing after them the hind-parts...everything becomes easy and graceful for the horse, because his forces being in perfect harmony, permit the rider to dispose of them in such a way that they mutually and constantly assist each other.

François Baucher *New Method of Horsemanship* (in *François Baucher, the Man and his Method*, by Hilda Nelson)

In a footnote to this passage, Baucher makes an interesting comment on conformation. A possible inference from this passage is

that less experienced horsemen of Baucher's era were attracted to horses whose faulty conformation seemed to mimic the lowered, engaged hindquarters of a horse correctly trained in advanced collection. For such riders, Baucher's observations are unequivocal:

I am not of the opinion of those connoisseurs who imagine that the qualities of the horse, as well as his speed in trotting, depend principally on the height of his withers. I think, that for the horse to be stylish and regular in his movements, the croup should be on a level with the withers; such was the construction of the old English horse...Horses with a low croup, or withers very high in proportion to their croup, are still in favor now-a-days among amateur horsemen. The German horses have an equally marked predilection for this sort of formation, although it is contrary to the strength of the croup, to the equilibrium of the horse, and to the regular play of his feet and legs. This fault of construction (for it is one)...is a great one, and really retards the horse's education. In fact we are obliged, in order to render his movements uniform, to lower his neck, so that the kind of lever it represents, may serve to lighten his hind-parts of the weight with which they are overburdened.

François Baucher *New Method of Horsemanship* (in *François Baucher, the Man and his Method,* by Hilda Nelson)

Like Baucher, Wynmalen also stresses the importance of balance:

The trot is a very important pace and we should aim at obtaining perfect balance at it. The amount of natural balance at this pace varies greatly from one horse to another...Balance at the trot will be obtained by making the horse trot quietly, at a steady and regular speed, which, combined with the continuous changes of direction, will cause the horse to shift back his centre of gravity, to use his quarters more energetically, to lift his head and neck, and to become 'lighter' in front. That in turn will result in higher and freer action, characteristic of the balanced trot.

Henry Wynmalen *Equitation*

Although some two hundred years separate their writing, there is a marked similarity between the exercises mentioned by Wynmalen and the following, from de la Guérinière's *School of Horsemanship:*

The trot, which is the fundamental lesson for rendering supple all types of horse, should rather be extended than raised in a hunting horse, so that the horse learns to extend its legs and shoulders freely. The bridoon is excellent for this purpose; with this instrument…the horse can be turned easily and without too much constraint…The horse should be trotted on both reins, without any thought to specific figures, but rather with great variety, turning it now to the right, now to the left on the circle, occasionally travelling on a straight line, longer or shorter according to whether the horse holds back or abandons itself too much to forward motion. The horse should be kept on the trot until it obeys the slightest movement of the rider's hand or leg and can turn easily on both reins.

François Robichon de la Guérinière *School of Horsemanship*

Although the term 'extended' is used here, this should perhaps be interpreted as being relative to the collected manège work that was still the 'norm' in de la Guérinière's era – the reference to carrying out the work in a bridoon may be significant here. Both de la Guérinière and Wynmalen are, essentially, talking about simple exercises to improve the horse's activity and balance in trot. This is another example of the timelessness of

de la Guérinière's writing; the passage remains entirely relevant to general trot work for the young horse, or to the riding-in of a mature animal.

Reiner Klimke, a Master of the modern era, makes the point that increasing the activity of the hindquarters requires skill and prudence:

We have to take some risks to develop the trot in the way we mean it to be developed. The rider must feel how much or how little he can ask.

In similar vein, Wilhelm Müseler emphasises that:

…it is most important never to lose the quiet, regular forward stride. When free forward movement can be maintained it is time to ask a little more of the horse, but immediately the free swing of the movement is lost we must realize that we have asked too much of him.   Wilhelm Müseler *Riding Logic*

Klimke goes on to describe an exercise aimed at producing and monitoring additional activity:

We can ask for a little more at the end of the session, when going along the long side in rising trot. We call this exercise 'lengthened trot'. The lengthening is created by a more active hind leg. We have to pay special attention at this stage to ensure that the steps do not become more hurried. If this happens we have to reduce the tempo (speed of the rhythm) with one or more half-halts and start again. We can repeat this several times to find out whether the horse has misunderstood us or hurries because its muscles are not strong enough to allow the strides to lengthen.

Reiner Klimke *Basic Training of the Young Horse*

While it is generally accepted that there are four main variants of trot – collected, working, medium and extended – it is, of course, possible to obtain further variations within these categories. The early lengthening described above is essentially a product of the working gait. John Winnett describes it in these terms:

Lengthening of the stride...is asked for in the beginning of training before the horse has gained sufficient suppleness and strength to perform the extended trot...the horse will cover as much ground per stride and show as much elasticity and suspension as his natural strength and cadence allow.

The lengthening of stride in trot is the first longitudinal exercise. The transitions should be asked for out of the working trot and back into the working trot...

John Winnett *Dressage as Art in Competition*

Waldemar Seunig describes how, at the appropriate stage, this basic lengthening of the stride can be married to a similar level of shortening:

Purpose: Confirmation of the horse's ability to balance himself, without losing rhythm in the changes of tempo. The stimulation of the impulsion and exuberance of the horse. The horse's yielding to controlling aids. Preparatory steps for achieving ultimate submission.

Lengthen the stride on the long side of the arena and shorten it on the short sides. This exercise should begin only when the horse has achieved a certain self-carriage...at the working trot and is able to balance himself under the weight of the rider. Should be done only for short periods...When working outdoors in open country, proceed on a straight line, preferably toward the stable, at a rising trot. Take advantage of the natural exuberance of the horse's way of going.

Aids: When lengthening the strides gradually increase the driving aids. Frequently ride with reins in one hand. When shortening the stride repeatedly increase the tension of the reins with a deep and engaged seat, but do not yet bring its...entire effect to bear.   Waldemar Seunig *The Essence of Horsemanship*

In *Horsemanship,* Seunig makes the observation:

Once the horse has advanced to the stage where contact with the bit at the working trot becomes more and more certain and positive as a result of careful driving, and it does not try to escape the bit, we can say that the horse is in hand, which means that it responds to the controls.

Waldemar Seunig *Horsemanship*

In other words, the working trot is now established. In an introductory passage to work on the gait variants, Henry Wynmalen describes a similar state of affairs:

...before we begin to talk of developing the trot [introducing the gait variants], we assume that the horse is capable of a good, unspoilt ordinary trot. That means a trot with reasonably roomy strides, of even length, in regular tempo and therefore of good rhythm; it means that the head be carried still, in a normal position, neither high nor low, with the nose in front of the vertical, at an angle of about 45°.

Henry Wynmalen *Dressage A Study of the Finer Points of Riding*

Schooling at the *Trot* alongside the wall
improves the action of the horse
and the firm position of
the rider.

Engraving from Johann Ridinger, reproduced in Albrecht's
A Dressage Judge's Handbook.

Further pointers to the desired qualities of the trot are given by Kurt Albrecht. In *A Dressage Judge's Handbook,* he lists some qualities of trot that should be evident in a horse working at Elementary level:

Moderate but perceptible cadence, resulting from regular two-time movement in diagonals and elasticity of the steps.

Freely maintained head position characteristic of horizontal equilibrium – the nose approaching the vertical...

A convexity of the upper border of the neck – due to proper development of the dorsal neck muscles and atrophy of the ventral ones – which ensures that the rein effects extend 'through' the body to the hindquarters.

A moderate elevation of the neck (an imaginary horizontal line must pass through the corners of the mouth and the hip joint).

In the corners of the arena and on all curves of the track the horse must be curved around the rider's inside leg to enable the hind feet to step in the traces of the fore feet: otherwise the hindquarters would deviate outwards and the inside fore would become overloaded.

The back must have attained a degree of elasticity sufficient to allow the rider to sit to the movement and maintain his balance easily.   Kurt Albrecht *A Dressage Judge's Handbook*

And, with specific reference to the working trot, Dr van Schaik writes:

It is too, up to the judges to stress in their commentary the importance of the engagement of the hindquarters. Without this engagement there will be no balanced rhythmic trot; there will be no pure gait.

Dr H.L.M. van Schaik *Misconceptions and Simple Truths in Dressage*

With a view to the end product, Alois Podhajsky provides both a technical description and a warning:

The brilliant trot depends on the suspension that the horse can produce. Suspension can only be achieved if the hindquarters produce a strong carrying and pushing force. The longer this moment of suspension lasts, the more beautiful and impressive will be the action of the horse. But the rider must beware of a false suspension in which the horse makes slow or false steps.

Alois Podhajsky   *The Complete Training of Horse and Rider*

Faults in the trot

In *The Complete Training of Horse and Rider*, **Alois Podhajsky makes two related points:**

The trot is the most important pace for the training of the horse and rider; faults that creep in at the trot will most likely have a bad influence on the other paces.

In the trot the rider has the best opportunity to control the regularity and the rhythm of the steps. The sensitive rider will immediately notice any irregularity in the pace and will change his work accordingly. The regularity of the tempo is the essence of training as it reflects the balance that the horse has acquired.

Alois Podhajsky *The Complete Training of Horse and Rider*

Outward signs of tractability and insufficient tractability, from Knopfhart's Dressage A Guidebook for the Road to Success.

However, if the rider is to discern and correct any irregularities in the trot, this presupposes first, a technical ability to do so, and second, that the rider's own actions are not contributing to the faulty steps. Podhajsky's former pupil, Charles Harris, writes:

If both the sitting and rising trot – and the transitions between them – are carried out correctly, the rider then has the ability to modify, and/or correct faulty equine locomotion...It is because many riders are not constant when trotting, i.e., rising too high, leaning too far forward, or falling backward, sometimes with a stiff posture, and other times with a slack body posture – or a combination of all these faults – which prevents them from improving the trot gait...   Charles Harris *Fundamentals of Riding*

Podhajsky goes on to describe various faulty actions in the trot:

One of the most common faults in the trot is the hurried steps of the forelegs in which they reach the ground before the diagonal hind leg, so that two separate hoof beats are heard instead of one. These horses carry a greater proportion of their weight and that of their rider on their shoulders. If the hind leg is put down before the diagonal foreleg and again two hoof beats are heard, it is known as a hasty hind leg. This fault will also occur when the horse does not bend his joints sufficiently and drags his hind legs along the ground. It is also a fault when the horse does not bring his hind legs sufficiently under his body and appears to make a longer stride with his forelegs, which accordingly have to be withdrawn to equal the stride of the hind legs. In terms of riding the horse promises more in front than he can show with his hindquarters. Another fault is when one hind leg steps more under the body than the other, thus making the strides uneven.

Alois Podhajsky *The Complete Training of Horse and Rider*

Trot in perfect diagonals of a ridden horse in acquired equilibrium. From Knopfhart's Fundamentals of Dressage.

The importance of true two-time movement is also emphasised by Erik Herbermann:

The presence of *diagonal unison* is of utmost importance. This means that, within the motion of any diagonal pair of legs, both legs must leave the ground (or alight on the ground again) at exactly the same moment. If the diagonal legs are not unified, an incorrect 3- or 4-beat motion results.

Erik Herbermann   Dressage Formula

While Ulrik Schramm warns against making additional demands of horses before existing faults have been corrected:

Horses that disconnect their trot must never be driven into a speedy trot before their topline has been lengthened, their back and shoulders loosened so that their forelimbs can make more ample gestures. And the first thing to attend to is the perfect regularity of the beat. Relative elevation, that is, a lowering of the hindquarters rather than an active elevation of the neck, results from flexion of all the joints of the hindquarters; this is what lightens the forehand, frees the shoulders, cadences the trot and expands the gestures of the forelimbs.

Ulrik Schramm   *The Undisciplined Horse*

Further faulty actions in trot are described by Üdo Burger who, in addition to being a great equestrian scholar, was also one of Germany's top equine veterinary surgeons.

Three striking examples of an impure trot are hovering, scurrying and bouncing. These are all actions which frequently impress the complete tyro, but experienced horsemen know how difficult it is to obtain, in the first place, genuine forward movement and, eventually, powerful collection and extension from horses that display these idiosyncrasies.

Hovering is a form of trotting in which a horse springs from one diagonal to the other without first properly flexing his hind joints; there is an upward thrust produced by the natural elasticity of muscles, tendons and ligaments, and a period of suspension, but no effective forward propulsion; the stride covers very little ground and, at the summit of its trajectory, the hindfeet do not point the toes toward the spot upon which they will land. The action is elevated, but stilted and ineffective; novice riders enjoy it because the resilience of the hindlegs allows them to sit on the horse's slack back as comfortably as in a rocking-chair. Horses that have got into the habit of hovering hate to change their speed; they feel insecure when they do so; they are like engines that heat-up as soon as a certain rate of revolutions is exceeded.

The scurrying trot is also a trot with stiffened hocks, but with the difference that there is no spring at all; the body is propelled forward by the rapidly alternating strokes of the diagonals; speed is gained by momentum as the mass is constantly projected over the forehand. In the scurrying trot, the hindlegs straddle; it is an action which is very difficult to correct.

The bouncing trot, on the other hand, is a bouncing off pronouncedly flexed hindlimbs with an explosive extension; the swing of the hindlegs is not sufficient to ensure effective forward propulsion. The limbs overwork, the back is rigidly hollowed, the neck held up; it is an action that is considered elegant in a carriage horse but which is highly unsuitable for a saddle-horse.

Burger also deals with that ultimate example of faulty trot, jogging:

Jogging is…usually linked to temperament. Jogging is trotting with such short steps that the jogging horse just manages to keep up with a walking horse. It can happen when an energetic horse with a long stride has to stay level with a slower horse and has to be continually slowed down; in this case, it is a vent for impatience. In contrast, a slow horse will jog to keep up with a longer striding companion. Jogging turns into a habit if the rider is inattentive or incompetent and, once the vice is established, it becomes almost impossible to get the horse to stretch the reins and to obey the aids. Jogging and hovering are related habits and it can be said that jogging is bridle-lameness on all four legs.

Correcting habitual jogging taxes severely the patience of the rider... one must be able to control the hindquarters and get them to produce normally long strides; a horse inexorably made to yield to the increased pressure of one leg cannot possibly jog; even when normal rein tension is re-established, the shoulder-in will have to be resorted to for a long time before the horse can be allowed to proceed on one track; the shoulder-in position and absolute obedience to the impelling influences of the legs will, eventually, enable one to nip in the bud any further attempts at jogging.　　　　　Üdo Burger *The Way to Perfect Horsemanship*

Down the years, a number of authorities have linked the hovering trot to a tense, tight back, so it is interesting that the veterinary surgeon, Burger, attributes it to incorrect action of the hind limbs. In *Exploring Dressage Technique*, Paul Belasik

The wrong way to sit on a jogging horse.

*Ulrik Schramm's sketch, 'The wrong way to sit on a jogging horse'
from* The Undisciplined Horse.

describes how he investigated the problem after he had observed it in three horses sent to him for training. Of one horse he writes:

The third horse had been trained to passage prematurely, obviously because it displayed a tendency towards exaggerated steps. The horse was a disaster when I tried longitudinal transitions. The elevation and stiffening got worse. In downward transitions the horse's hind end bounced up and down like an empty wagon on a rough road.

In seeking a remedy, Belasik undertook a detailed study of the biomechanics of trot. Initially, he was mindful of the 'tight back'

Tense trot, ineffective aids.
From Knopfhart's Fundamentals of Dressage.

Horse above the bit, set at the poll and rigid in the back.
From Knopfhart's Fundamentals of Dressage.

theory, but this did not seem to tie in with his observations:
For one thing, none of my hovering horses had a particularly
tight back…In fact, two were long in the back and flexible. The
other interesting matter was that all three horses were lazy in
their way of going and manner.

**Detailed research into the actions of the limbs during trot drew
Belasik's attention to the stifle, hock and shoulder:**

In that third hovering horse…it was precisely a lack of muscular
effort in flexing the stifle and shoulder that produced the verti-

cal bounding of the hover trot. In the stance phase up front, the knee is locked, so all dampening and changing has to occur in the joint of the scapula and humerus. Likewise, in the stance phase of the rear leg, the hock, until it extends, is fairly locked and braced, so all the dampening and changing has to occur in the stifle and hip. When the horse fails to flex the joints in the stifle, the superficial flexor tendon in the rear leg can't loosen when the hock extends and the fetlock raises against the tightened tendon. The result is that the hips are bounced upward. When this is repeated step after step the horse's centre of gravity bounces up and down with a much diminished forward impulse. What you get is hovering.

These findings led Belasik to conclude that a tight, tense back, was not the *fundamental* source of the hovering trot:

...a tight back facilitates the hovering steps, but...the action of the back...is secondary to the action of the legs. Power must first be generated before the back can react to it. The action of the back cannot produce any steps at all, elastic or 'exalted and exaggerated'. The action of the legs, and more specifically the muscular action of the shoulder, stifle and hock, must produce swift, strong, forward impulsive movement. The inaction of the legs, and more specifically the muscular inaction of the shoulder, stifle and hock, produces hovering steps...

The hovering trot is a muscular problem. Like most ways of going, predisposition to it is probably genetic. However, the trainer can make headway if he realises the sites at which the work must take place: namely, the stifle, hip, hock and shoulder. Then he needs to apply creatively the traditional exercises to develop flexibility and strength in those areas...

Longitudinal flexing exercises, such as the series of transitions...can work, if the rider can get the horse to work the joints of the hind leg and set the balance more toward the rear. However, if...the movement has become habitual, and the inflexibility of the stifle is really confirmed, then transitions will not be very effective...

Much more effective is the use of proper lateral exercises, in particular the shoulder-in but also the renvers and half-pass. The shoulder-in has great value as a unilateral exercise. In the left shoulder-in, the rider/trainer can work specifically on the joints of the left hind and this specific loading can make a particularly stiff leg more flexible. Also by working one side at a time in a curve, the rider can arrest the attempt of the horse to stiffen the back... I don't want to minimise the importance of the back.

Paul Belasik *Exploring Dressage Technique*

Perhaps the fundamental lesson to be learnt from observations such as this is that, when a horse does not comply correctly with the rider's requirements, the root cause may be far more complex than simple 'disobedience'.

Conclusion

For most riders, further work on the trot will entail development of the gait variants. In addition to the working trot, these are generally accepted nowadays as being medium, collected and extended trot – the definitions currently used by the FEI – although a number of Masters, including the late Nuno Oliveira, have identified far more variants than these.

Collection and extension, which are subjects for another title in this series, cannot be pursued successfully unless the basic form of the gait is correct. This is a major reason – in addition to its inherent schooling value – why the Masters place so much emphasis on the development of a good, pure working trot.

In today's competitive world, it is probably true to say that many people view the gait variants fundamentally in terms of progression through the test levels. Therefore, in concluding this book, and by way of providing a stepping stone to the gait variants, it may be instructive to consider Waldemar Seunig's description of medium trot, not as a test movement, but as a valuable schooling gait which may, in the right circumstances, be introduced at quite an early stage of the horse's education:

If after about nine months of training, the young horse's croup, back and stomach muscles have become strengthened, and the impulsion of the hindquarters and their capacity for flexing developed by the bending exercises are assured, the medium trot can be practised for short periods.

The medium trot is an intensification of the working trot with respect to ground coverage...carriage and expression; and is in the middle between collected and extended trot...

The medium trot is not a working gait, but as a schooling gait and an aid to the gymnastic development it is essential...

Purpose: The improvement of the gait by means of extending thrust and impulsion. Stabilizing the balance, carriage and posture of the horse by means of greater engagement of the hindquarters with resulting flexion of the neck and poll. Confident obedience to the aids.

Waldemar Seunig *The Essence of Horsemanship*

Bibliography

Many of the books cited in this work have been produced in numerous editions, sometimes by more than one publisher. Some, indeed, have been subject to various translations into different languages. Listed below are the editions which have been referred to during the compilation of this book. Where appropriate, information on first publication has been added, to help place the works in historical context.

Albrecht, Kurt, *A Dressage Judge's Handbook*, J.A. Allen (London) 1988.

Baucher, François, *New Method of Horsemanship,* in *François Baucher the Man and his Method,* Hilda Nelson, J.A. Allen (London) 1992. (First published as *Méthode d'Equitation basée sur de nouveaux principes,* France 1842.)

Belasik, Paul, *Exploring Dressage Technique,* J.A. Allen (London) 1994.

Burger, Üdo, *The Way to Perfect Horsemanship* (tr. Nicole Bartle), J.A. Allen (London) 1998. (First published as *Vollendete Reitkunst,* Paul Parey, Berlin and Hamburg 1959.)

Decarpentry, Gen., *Academic Equitation* (tr. Nicole Bartle), J.A. Allen (London) 1987. (First published in France 1949).

De la Guérinière, François Robichon, *School of Horsemanship* (tr. Tracy Boucher), J.A. Allen (London) 1994. (First published in a single volume as *Ecole de Cavalerie*, Paris 1733.)

d'Endrödy, Lt. Col. A.L., *Give Your Horse a Chance*, J.A. Allen (London) 1989 (First edn. 1959).

Felton, W. Sidney, *Masters of Equitation*, J.A. Allen (London) 1962.

Fillis, James, *Breaking and Riding*, J.A. Allen (London) 1986. (First English Edition 1902.)

Harris, Charles, *Fundamentals of Riding*, J.A. Allen (London) 1985.

Herbermann, Erik, *Dressage Formula* (3rd edn.), J.A. Allen (London) 1999.

Klimke, Reiner, *Basic Training of the Young Horse* (tr. Sigrid Young), J.A. Allen (London) 1994. (First published as *Grundausbildung des jungen Reitpferdes*, Franckh'sche Verlagshandlung, Stuttgart 1984.)

Knopfhart, Alfred, *Fundamentals of Dressage*, (tr. Nicole Bartle) J.A. Allen (London) 1990. (First published as *Grundlagen des Dressurreitens*, Paul Parey, Berlin and Hamburg 1979.)

L'Hotte, Gen. Alexis-François, *Questions Équestres* (tr. Hilda Nelson in *Alexis-François L'Hotte The Quest For Lightness In Equitation)*, J.A. Allen (London) 1997. (*Questions Équestres* first published in France, 1906.)

Müseler, Wilhelm, *Riding Logic* (tr. F.W. Schiller), Eyre Methuen Ltd. (London) 1975. (First published as *Müseler: REITLEHRE*, Paul Parey Verlag, Berlin and Hamburg pre. 1937.)

Oliveira, Nuno, *Reflections on Equestrian Art* (tr. Phyllis Field), J.A. Allen (London) 1988. (First published as *Reflexions sur l'Art Equestre*, Crépin Leblond, France 1964.)

Notes and Reminiscences of a Portuguese Rider, special publication 1982.

Podhajsky, Alois, *The Complete Training of Horse and Rider* (tr. Eva Podhajsky), The Sportsman's Press (London) 1997. (First published as *Die Klassiche Reitkunst*, Nymphenburger Verlagshand-lung GmbH., Munich 1965.)

Schramm, Ulrik, *The Undisciplined Horse* (tr. Nicole Bartle), J.A. Allen (London) 1986. (First published as *Das verrittene Pferd – Ursachen und Weg der Korrektur,* BLV Verlagsgesellschaft, Munich 1983.)

Seunig, Waldemar, *Horsemanship* (tr. Leonard Mins), Robert Hale (London) 1958. (First published in Germany 1941.)

The Essence of Horsemanship (tr. Jacqueline Stirlin Harris), J.A. Allen (London) 1986. (First published in Germany by Erich Hoffmann Verlag 1961.)

Steinbrecht, Gustav, *The Gymnasium of the Horse* (tr. from German 10th edn. Helen K. Buckle), Xenophon Press (Cleveland Heights, OH, USA) 1995. (First published in Germany 1885.)

van Schaik, Dr H.L.M., *Misconceptions and Simple Truths in Dressage,* J.A. Allen (London) 1986.

Wätjen, Richard L., *Dressage Riding* (tr. Dr V. Saloschin), J.A. Allen (London) 1973. (First published in Germany 1958.)

Winnett, John, *Dressage as Art in Competition,* J.A. Allen (London) 1993.

Wynmalen, Henry, *Dressage A Study of the Finer Points of Riding,* Wilshire Book Company (North Hollywood, CA, USA) (First published in 1952.)

Equitation, J.A. Allen (London) 1971. (First edn.1938.)

Biographies of Quoted Masters

The following are brief biographies of those whose works are cited in this book. They are given both for reasons of general interest and to assist the reader in placing each author in historical and cultural context.

Albrecht, Kurt Born in Austria in 1920, Albrecht chose a military career and saw active service as an Artillery Commander in the Second World War, before becoming a prisoner of war in Russia. After the war, he joined the Austrian Constabulary and taught equitation at the Constabulary Central School.

Albrecht was a great friend of Hans Handler and, when Handler succeeded Alois Podhajsky as Director of the Spanish Riding School, Albrecht joined the School to assist with administration, being appointed Substitute Director in 1965. In 1974 he succeeded Handler as Director, a post he held until 1985.

From 1973 until 1987 Albrecht was in charge of judges' affairs for the Austrian Equestrian Federation, subsequently playing a leading role in equestrian educational advancement.

Baucher, François (1796–1873) A highly controversial figure, who rode entirely in the school, Baucher began his career under the tutelage of his uncle, director of stables to the

Governor of Milan. Whilst in Italy, he would have witnessed the practices of the old Neapolitan school, which were still dominant in that country.

In 1816, political upheaval saw Baucher's return to France, where he managed and taught in several private manèges. In 1834, he moved to Paris and established a relationship with the fashionable Franconi circus. Riding haute école in the circus gave Baucher the prestige he yearned, and in 1842 he published his 'new method' *(Méthode d'Equitation basée sur de nouveaux principes).*

In 1855, Baucher was badly injured when the chandelier of an indoor school fell on him. Thereafter, he never performed in public again, although he remained able to do some riding and teaching. In later life, he became very reflective and appears to have modified some of his earlier ideas.

The controversy that surrounded Baucher's writing and teaching is well documented in Hilda Nelson's *François Baucher the Man and his Method,* in which the author writes: 'The goal of Baucher's method is the total disposition of the horse's strength and the total submission of the horse to the will of the horseman.' What is beyond question is that Baucher trained a number of dangerous horses to perform advanced movements in a remarkably short time, and Fillis said of him: 'He had the great merit of not describing anything which he could not do.'

Baucher remains respected by many eminent authorities and his reputation is believed by some to have been compromised by equestrian politics, the limitations of his own powers of expression, and the insensitivity of his translators.

Belasik, Paul Born in Buffalo, New York in 1950, Belasik showed a strong affinity with animals from childhood. Early interests included monkey breeding and falconry, as well as horses. This diversity of interest extended beyond the animal kingdom – entering Cornell University as part of the pre-veterinary programme, he graduated with a science degree and had, in the meantime, won prizes for his painting and become a published poet.

By the time of his graduation in 1971, Belasik's career as a horseman had already begun; he taught college courses, evented and competed in dressage at all levels. However, never really excited by competition, he began to focus more on an in-depth study of equitation for its own sake. Initially involved in breeding and training German horses, he focused first upon the German system, broadening and deepening his studies to encompass the different schools of riding. He cites as major influences H.L.M. van Schaik, who instilled in him a love of the classicists and Nuno Oliveira, with whom he spent some time in Portugal. His interest in the philosophical aspects of equitation has been augmented by studies of Zen Buddhism and the martial arts.

Belasik owns and operates a training stable in Pennsylvania, where he works with a broad-based clientele including international competitors, and riders of all levels who have no interest in competition. He also holds clinics and lectures on a national and international basis.

Burger, Üdo (1914–1980) One of Germany's most respected veterinary surgeons and animal psychologists, Burger was an accomplished horseman and a highly respected judge. Involved with horses from an early age, he was reputed to become fretful if unable to spend some time each day in their company. Very obviously a horse lover, he wrote (without giving specific detail) that a horse had actually saved his life in wartime. His professional skills gave him a profound understanding of both the horse's movement and motivation, and he could be blunt in his criticism of rough riding, and of those who made insufficient effort to understand the horse's nature.

Decarpentry, General (1878–1956) Born at Lambres, the son and grandson of enthusiastic pupils of François Baucher, Decarpentry soon decided upon a career in the cavalry. Wounded in action at Verdun, he dismissed the permanent damage to his left elbow, saying that it kept his arm bent in the correct position for riding. The injury had no adverse affect on his career, since he was to become commander of cavalry at Saint-Cyr and second in command of the Cadré Noir (1925–31).

From 1939 onward, Decarpentry acted as judge at many international dressage competitions. He also presided over the FEI jury and became President of the FEI Dressage Committee, in which role he was highly influential in developing an international consensus on the aims and judging of competition dressage.

As a rider and equestrian thinker, Decarpentry was by no means confined by the Baucheriste influences of his childhood, as both the references cited in *Academic Equitation,* and his own text shows. It is also evident that he took innovative advantage of the then-young techniques of cinematography to help analyse equine movement.

Decarpentry was a modest man and, although held in great esteem as a rider, he had no desire to participate in competition, his legacy being the skill of his instruction, his work in developing the FEI and the integrity and scholarship which he applied to his equestrian writing.

De la Guérinière, François Robichon (c.1688–1751) Widely regarded as the most influential figure in equestrian history, de la Guérinière was born in Essay, the son of a lawyer. A pupil of Antoine de Vendeuil, he also had a brother who ran a riding academy in Caen. In 1715, de la Guérinière was granted the title of *écuyer de roi,* and opened a riding academy in Paris, apparently under licence from the Duc d'Anjou.

At his Parisian academy, de la Guérinière taught not only riding, but what was described as 'the complete science of the horse'. By 1730 his reputation was such that he was given the Directorship of the Académie des Tuileries. Despite phenomenal success as a teacher, de la Guérinière was unable to run the academy profitably, and struggled constantly with money – a fact which might endear him to modern-day equestrians.

De la Guérinière's legacy was to develop, from the older style of classical riding, a freedom of movement which characterises modern classical equitation – an achievement which has led him to be described as the 'first of the modern classical riders' (W.S. Felton) and 'undoubtedly the father of modern equitation' (Wynmalen). His lucid work *Ecole de Cavalerie* is quite remarkable for its timeless relevance and wisdom, and continues to be a source of reference for many present-day authorities.

d'Endrödy, Lt. Col. A.L. (1902–1988) A native of Hungary, a country with a great equestrian heritage, d'Endrödy was a member of the Royal Hungarian Olympic three-day event team in 1936, a member of the Hungarian international showjumping team and a champion amateur race rider. The basic idea for *Give Your Horse a Chance* was formulated during the fourteen years which d'Enrödy spent at Orkenytabor, the Hungarian Academy for riding instructors and the training ground for their Olympic team. The book itself was drafted during the three and a half ('sad, lonely') years in which he was a prisoner of war in Russian hands, and it may be that the depth of detail in the book is partially attributable to this period of incarceration.

One of d'Endrödy's major influences was as the trainer of Bertalan de Nemethy, coach to the USA Olympic equestrian team in a golden era that produced riders such as William Steinkraus – a great equestrian scholar, who helped refine the translation of *Give Your Horse a Chance* and provided the preface. Largely through his meeting with Col. Frank Weldon at the Stockholm Olympics (where Weldon captained the victorious British Team), d'Endrödy also had a considerable impact on equitation in Britain and spent some time at Badminton, as a guest of the Duke of Beaufort.

Felton, W. Sidney The author of the informative work quoted in the preliminary pages of this book, Felton was born in Massachusetts in 1895. A graduate of Harvard Law School, he served as a US Aviation Officer in the First World War, and subsequently practised law in Boston. A lifelong rider and highly analytical equestrian scholar, he was a keen follower of hounds, an amateur instructor and judge and a leading figure in the organisation of the US Pony Club. Felton was well respected by many leading riders of his era, and the foreword for his *Masters of Equitation* was provided by Henry Wynmalen.

Fillis, James (1834–1913) Born in London, Fillis went to France at an early age. There he met François Baucher and, greatly impressed by his methods, studied them under Baucher's pupil, François Caron. (Later in life, Fillis found himself at odds with some of Baucher's ideas – as his *Commentaries on Baucher* in *Breaking and Riding* show – but he always retained an overall admiration for him.)

After running his own school in Le Havre, Fillis moved to Paris, where he supervised the stables of various members of the nobility. Then, wishing to promote his method more widely, he followed the same course as Baucher, and began to perform in the circus, to great acclaim. Pressed to produce a book, Fillis was offered editorial assistance by a long-time pupil, the French politician, Clemenceau. Published in 1890, the book was subsequently translated into English by the eminent veterinary author, Horace Hayes.

From 1891–7, Fillis was based in Germany. He then went to Russia with Circus Ciniselli and created such an impression that he was offered, and accepted, the post of Colonel and *Ecuyer-en-chef* of the Russian Cavalry School – a position he held until retiring in 1910. During his period of office, a visiting American Army Commission decided to adopt his method, and *Breaking and Riding* became the official textbook of the US Cavalry School.

Interestingly, given that he was active only a century or so ago, Fillis totally disapproved of women riding astride!

Harris, Charles (b. 1915) An engineer by profession, Charles Harris qualified as a riding instructor in 1932 and went on to become a Fellow of the Institute of the Horse, a Fellow of the British Horse Society and a Fellow of the Association of British Riding Schools.

From 1948–51, through the support of Col. V.D.S. Williams, he became the first and only English rider to complete the full three-year course at the Spanish Riding School. Here, he trained under Commandants Alois Podhajsky and Hans

Handler, and with such luminaries as Rochowansky, Lindenbauer and Wahl.

A fervent devotee of classical principles, Charles Harris is an advocate of using correct equestrian terminology to ensure that these principles are conveyed precisely and concisely to pupils and students of equitation, and his many writings reflect this fact.

Herbermann, Erik Born in Amsterdam in 1945, Herbermann moved at an early age with his family to Johannesburg and ten years later, moved to Canada. His initial equestrian training was with Patricia Salt FBHS, herself a pupil of Richard Wätjen and Oberbereiter Lindenbauer at the Spanish Riding School. Herbermann subsequently studied under the celebrated classical riding teacher, Egon von Neindorff.

Now residing in the USA, Herbermann devotes much of his time to lecturing, teaching and conducting clinics internationally. As well as producing three editions of *Dressage Formula*, he has also written numerous articles for equestrian publications.

Herbermann is a staunch advocate of classical ideals, and his ideology is based on an objective study of the horse's nature, which seeks the depth of understanding and quality of work perceived in the greatest of Renaissance Masters. In common with these luminaries, he views equitation as a self-improving art, rooted in the utmost affection and respect for the horse.

Klimke, Reiner (1936–1999) Born in Munster, Germany, Klimke began his association with horses when, evacuated to a farm during the war years, he journeyed to school by horse and cart. After the war, he took lessons at Herr Stecken's

Westphalian Riding School and, in 1953, he came to the notice of Gustav Rau, who did much to revive Germany's equestrian fortunes in the post-war era. Rau invited Klimke to train at Warendorf, where for three years his roommate was the great showjumper, Alwin Schockemöhle. At that time Schockemöhle was concentrating on eventing but, in 1956, he decided that his future lay in showjumping, and passed the ride on his horse, Lausbub, to Klimke – who promptly won team silver at the 1957 European Three Day Event Championships. Two years later, Klimke won team gold at these championships on Fortunat.

By this time, Klimke was also achieving considerable success in dressage, and his career was under way. Having studied law from 1955, he became a fully qualified lawyer in 1964. With the demands of his profession to consider, he decided that he could more readily combine this with his equestrian activities if he concentrated upon dressage rather than eventing. This decision saw the start of a long and immensely successful period of international competition revolving mainly, but not exclusively, around the great horses Dux, Mehmed and Ahlerich. During a period spanning three decades Klimke, as an individual, won an Olympic gold medal, two World Championships and four European Championships, and was a member of teams that won Germany gold medals at six Olympics, six World Championships and thirteen European Championships.

Knopfhart, Alfred Born in Vienna in 1927, Knopfhart studied economics and business administration, graduating in these subjects in 1951. Having begun riding in Austria at the age of nineteen, he then went to Germany to continue his equestrian studies. In 1962 he became a certified teacher of riding, and was awarded the German silver medal for riders. Since that time, he has worked continually as a trainer of horses and riders at all levels up to Grand Prix and, since 1989, has given annual clinics at several dressage centres in the USA.

In 1964, Knopfhart became a certified judge for dressage, showjumping and eventing; in 1968 an official of the Austrian Horse Show Association and in 1970 an international FEI dressage judge. From 1986–96, he headed the official body of Austrian show judges.

In addition to lecturing at the University of Veterinary Medicine, Vienna, Knopfhart has written three books and many articles on equestrian issues.

L'Hotte, Gen. Alexis-François (1825–1904) A son and grandson of French cavalrymen, L'Hotte was, from an early age, a keen student of the equestrian writings of the old French Masters – much to the detriment of his academic education. He initially attended the military academy of Saint-Cyr as a young cadet, being sent on to pursue his equestrian interests at Saumur, since the cavalry section at Saint-Cyr had been closed. Despite some youthful indiscipline, he eventually attained the rank of General, and became Commandant of the re-opened cavalry section at Saint-Cyr, and subsequently of Saumur.

It is of great interest to students of equestrian history that L'Hotte was a pupil of both François Baucher and Comte D'Aure, two highly influential figures who not only practised different styles of equitation, but were considered rivals and had their own factions of supporters. L'Hotte was a great notetaker, and his anecdotes about and comparisons of these two figures make fascinating reading.

L'Hotte himself was considered to be one of the most out-standing *écuyers* of a golden age: he originated the phrase 'equestrian tact' and the famous maxim 'calm, forward and straight'.

Müseler, Wilhelm (1887–1952) Born in Berlin, Müseler was, in his youth, a fine athlete – he held the German record for the 100m sprint. Following a grammar school education, he embarked upon a career as a cavalry officer. During the years preceding the First World War, he competed with great suc-cess at dressage and showjumping, and was a member of the German Olympic equestrian team. However, upon being told by his commanding officer that he should make his career 'with his intellect rather than his backside', he intensified his com-mitment to his primary role as an officer. His military abilities are evidenced by the fact that, by 1918, he had become the youngest Major on the General Staff. Later in life, when recalled to the General Staff at the onset of World War II, he was to attain the rank of General.

Leaving the army after the end of the First World War, Müseler again committed himself to equitation, becoming Director of Tattersall Beermann, then the largest equestrian centre in Berlin. In this role, his emphasis shifted away from active competition and towards training horses and riders and organising equestrian events. He also became Master of the Berlin Hunting Society and President of the German Association of Hunting Clubs.

In 1931, health problems compelled him to cease his riding activities. *Riding Logic,* written by way of a conclusion, was orig-inally intended for the academic equestrian societies he had founded. Once published, however, the book became a best-seller, appearing in many editions and many languages. From

1932 onward, Müseler also wrote books on the history of art, one of which sold over a million copies – he considered these books the most important work of his life.

Oliveira, Nuno (d. 1989) This great Portuguese Master began his career as a pupil of Joaquin Gonzales de Miranda, former Master of the Horse to the Portuguese Royal Family. After Miranda's death, Oliveira trained horses first for cavalry officers and a dealer, then for one of Miranda's pupils, Senōr Chefalenez. Subsequently, a friend and student, Manuel de Barros asked him to train at his brother-in-law's stud where, in addition to having many good horses to ride, he also had at his disposal a large equestrian library. During this period, he met Alois Podhajsky when they both rode at an exhibition in the Campo Grande and the pair became firm friends.

During the 1950s, Oliveira attracted a number of highly talented pupils, and opened his riding school at Quinta do Chafaris. He also began to write articles (and subsequently, books) on equitation, while a pupil organised a weekly TV programme showing his lessons.

In 1961 he gave his first exhibition abroad, in Switzerland, and the following year he rode in the Winter Circus in Paris, where he met and established a lasting relationship with Capt. Durand, later to be Commander of the Cadre Noir.

Subsequent years saw a further influx of pupils, many from abroad, and numerous clinics and exhibitions throughout Europe, North and South America and Australia, which continued up to the time of his death.

Podhajsky, Alois (1899–1973) The son of an Austro-Hungarian cavalry officer, Podhajsky joined a dragoon regiment aged seventeen and received regular lessons from Capt. Count

Telekei, whom he described as an excellent instructor.

Although in a cavalry regiment, Podhajsky spent much of the First World War on foot. After the war, following the demise of the Austro-Hungarian Empire, he was admitted to the new Federal Army, and riding once again became part of his career. Having achieved considerable success in showjumping, he was encouraged by his colonel to study dressage, which he found further improved his horse's jumping. Transferred to advanced training at the cavalry school at Schlosshof, he began to achieve international success in dressage, showjumping and three-day events.

In 1933, he was sent to the Spanish Riding School, where he studied under luminaries such as Polak, Zrust and Lindenbauer. Their influence helped him to train his own horses to Grand Prix level and to win a bronze medal for dressage at the 1936 Olympics.

From 1934–8 he worked as a cavalry instructor, first in Austria and then in Germany. In 1938 Austria was annexed by Germany, and the Spanish Riding School was placed under the command of the German Army. When, in 1939, Podhajsky became Director of the Spanish Riding School, he managed to convince senior German officers, who were experienced horsemen, of the value of the School. By this, and other actions in that period, Podhajsky was instrumental in protecting the School for posterity.

In the post-war years, Podhajsky competed abroad both with his own horses and the School's Lipizzaners. He also took the Spanish Riding School on a number of foreign tours, including a major tour of the USA shortly before his retirement in 1964.

Schramm, Ulrik (1912–1995) A vastly experienced German horseman and equestrian author, who was dedicated to the proper education of horses for all disciplines. His philosophy is expounded in his own words: 'Seat is obviously an essential element in mastery of the horse, but the rider's head is surely as important as his seat'; 'Riding is not truly a sport if unity of mind does not exist between rider and horse.' A talented artist, Schramm used his own mild caricatures of horses and riders to emphasise the points made in his writing.

Seunig, Waldemar (1887–1976) Born in the then Duchy of Krain, Seunig was educated at a military academy in Austria and entered the cavalry. He subsequently attended the Riding Instructors' Institute in Vienna, where he became a pupil of the famous Josipovich. Then, in the political upheaval of the times, he was more or less repatriated (to what was by that time Slovenia, in Yugoslavia).

Since, by then, he had established a considerable reputation, he was offered the post of Master of the Horse at the Yugoslavian Royal Court. This he accepted, on condition that he first spent a year at the French Cavalry School at Saumur, and six months at the Royal Mews in London (to learn protocol). Subsequently, he was also granted a year at the Spanish Riding School, back in Vienna.

Following a decline of royal interest in riding, Seunig became Chief Riding Master of the Yugoslavian Cavalry School in 1930. However, when offered promotion to General, he retired instead, since this would have entailed active service for a country for which he had no patriotic feelings.

After this retirement he kept riding, and, an Olympic competitor himself, also coached the German team that was successful in the Berlin Olympics. When, during the Second World War, Slovenian partisans destroyed his home, he moved to Germany where he gained high office as an equestrian instructor in the army.

After the war, he travelled extensively and became renowned as a rider, teacher and international judge. A great lover of literature, Seunig was also a keen artist and many of his own drawings adorn his books.

Steinbrecht, Gustav (1808–1885) Born in Saxony, Steinbrecht studied veterinary medicine before becoming a pupil of Louis Seeger, one of the most influential trainers of the nineteenth century, who had, himself, been a pupil of Weyrother, a celebrated figure of the Spanish Riding School.

Steinbrecht stayed with Seeger for eight years, during which time he married Seeger's niece and became an accomplished *écuyer*. He then took over direction of a manège in Magdeburg, where he remained for a further eight years, before rejoining Seeger.

In 1849, Steinbrecht became director of Seeger's establishment and, at about this time, began to make the notes that were to form the basis of *The Gymnasium of the Horse*. Seeger himself disagreed with the teachings of François Baucher – also active at this time – preferring methods and principles expounded by de la Guérinière. That Steinbrecht shared Seeger's view of Baucher is obvious from the vigorous attacks upon Baucher's method which permeate *The Gymnasium of the Horse*.

As Steinbrecht's health failed, he entrusted the completion of his book to his pupil/disciple, Paul Plinzer. Through Plinzer, and Plinzer's eminent pupil, Hans von Heydebreck, the work of Steinbrecht had a major influence on the formulation of the German [army] Riding Rules, and on German equitation in general.

van Schaik, Dr H.L.M. (1899–1991) Born in Holland, Dr van Schaik began his riding career as a showjumper. In this discipline, he represented his country many times with conspicuous success: in 1936 he was a member of the team that won silver at the Berlin Olympics. Gradually, however, his interest turned more and more towards dressage.

After the war, he settled in the USA, where he opened a riding academy and became highly respected as a rider, trainer and judge. Throughout the 1960s, 70s and 80s, he was one of a number of riders from the classical mould who were increasingly concerned that competition dressage was departing from classical principles. His book *Misconceptions and Simple Truths in Dressage* has its roots in articles he wrote to try to reverse that trend.

Wätjen, Richard L. Born in 1891, early backing from his parents enabled Wätjen to embark upon a career devoted entirely to equitation – and he did not squander this privileged position. After studying at Trakehen and Graditz, both German government studs, he spent six years (1916–21) as a pupil of the Spanish Riding School, then stayed on for a further six years as a guest amateur instructor and trainer.

In 1925, he moved to Berlin and began training horses and riders on a professional basis. This scheme proved highly successful: his pupils achieved great national and international success, and he was instrumental in training several Olympic teams, including the British team which competed at Helsinki in 1952.

As a rider, he produced many horses of various breeds to the highest standards, and achieved international success competing in both dressage and showjumping, two of his best-known horses being Burgsdorff and Wotan. Many authorities regard him as being one of the most elegant riders of his era.

Winnett, John Born in Los Angeles in 1928, Winnett was educated in Paris, where he was introduced to riding in the French classical tradition by Victor Laurent, a retired officer from Saumur who had studied under the doctrine of L'Hotte. Winnett subsequently became interested in showjumping and was instructed according to the methods of Col. Danloux, who had refined principles introduced by Federico Caprilli. He became French Junior National Champion in 1945.

As an adult Winnett 'abandoned serious riding to pursue a career' in the Indian sub-continent, Europe and subsequently New York. This 'abandonment' did not prevent him from amateur race-riding, playing polo and, indeed, representing the USA in the 1952 World Showjumping Championships.

Retiring early from a successful career, Winnett turned his full concentration upon horses and went to Germany, to study with Reiner Klimke. In Germany, he was initially surprised to discover a very free-moving style of equitation which traced back to the teachings of de la Guérinière. Much influenced by these German methods, to which he added a detailed study of equine biomechanics, Winnett achieved great success in competition dressage, becoming riding captain of the American team at the 1972 Olympics and continuing to represent his country at the highest levels throughout the 1970s and 1980s.

Wynmalen, Henry (1889–1964) Undoubtedly one of the most influential figures in British equitation, Wynmalen was Dutch by birth and spent his early life in Holland, coming to England in 1927. An engineer by profession, Wynmalen's many interests included yachting, motor rallying and aviation. A flying accident, which left a legacy of back trouble, resulted in Wynmalen adopting a somewhat individualistic riding posture, but did not prevent him from being a consummate all-round horseman.

His early years were devoted primarily to showjumping, cross-country riding and racing, and he was, for many years, MFH to the Woodland Hunt. Always concerned with the correct schooling of horses, and renowned for his quiet, patient methods, he became increasingly interested in classical dressage. In 1948, he won the British Dressage Championship, and followed this with many other successes. His displays at the Royal Windsor Show, and the ease with which his 'dressage' horses performed across country, served to ignite a greater interest in dressage in Britain – an interest he helped to promote with no reduction in his enthusiasm for the other disciplines.

A highly successful breeder and exhibitor of show horses, a respected judge and President of the Arab Horse Society, Wynmalen also served on the Executive Council of the BHS. Largely responsible for organising the horse trials competition at the 1948 (London) Olympics, he played a major role in instigating one-day events and, for some years, served as President of the Jury at Badminton horse trials.